THE
MICROCOMPUTER
THE
SCHOOL LIBRARIAN
AND THE
TEACHER
an introduction with case studies

THE
MICROCOMPUTER
THE
SCHOOL LIBRARIAN
AND THE
TEACHER

an introduction with case studies

edited by

JAMES E HERRING
Lecturer in Librarianship and Information Studies,
Robert Gordon's Institute of Technology

CLIVE BINGLEY  LONDON

© The contributors, 1987

Published by
Clive Bingley Limited
7 Ridgmount Street
London WC1E 7AE

First published 1987

British Library Cataloguing in Publication Data
Herring, James E.
    The microcomputer, the school librarian and the teacher.
    1. School libraries — Data processing
    3. Microcomputers — Library applications
    I. Title
027.8'028'5416   Z675.S3

ISBN 0-85157-399-1

Typeset by Style Photosetting Ltd, Tunbridge Wells, Kent.
Printed and made in England by Dotesios Printers Ltd,
Bradford-on-Avon, Wiltshire.

Contents

Acknowledgements

I would like to thank all the contributors for their excellent chapters but thanks must also go to others who helped: Rachel Mathieson who illustrated Chapter 1; Chapter 2 – Carol Stewart, Lynda Bain, Margaret O'Shea, Julie Innis and Jean Beck; Chapter 3 – Yvonne Low and Neville Wood; Chapter 4 – Les Rae; Chapter 5 – Audrey Nolan, Ann Johnston and Lynda Bain; Chapter 7 – Nigel Akers; Chapter 8 – Jenny Brown; Chapter 10 – David Coleman; Appendix 1 – David Andrews; Appendix 3 – Ann Irving.

Love and thanks also to Val, Jonathan and Stuart who lost part of the holidays.

James E Herring

Contributors

James E Herring is lecturer in the School of Librarianship and Information Studies, Robert Gordon's Institute of Technology, Aberdeen.

Renee Deans is school librarian at Falmer High School, Brighton.

Dorothy Williams is Research Assistant, School of Librarianship and Information Studies, Robert Gordon's Institute of Technology, Aberdeen.

Sandra Davison is school librarian, Milne's High School, Fochabers.

Jan Condon is librarian, Solihull Sixth form College, Solihull.

Judith Askey is school librarian, Houghton Regis Upper School, Houghton Regis.

Virginia Berkeley, formerly County Youth Librarian, Bedfordshire Libraries, now works with ILEA.

Bill Paton is Regional Librarian, Grampian Region School Library Service, Aberdeen.

Introduction
by James E Herring

The developments in microcomputing in education and elsewhere in recent years has been staggering. It is easy to forget that even five years ago, there was little to be offered to education in the way of cheap, efficient microcomputers and directly usable software. The pace of change in this area means that hardware purchased today becomes instantly obsolescent. This book is not about hardware and the technical features of microcomputers, although a basic guide is included, but is set firmly in the use of microcomputers as educational tools which can add new dimensions to present-day education.

The emphasis throughout the book will be on 'information' and not technology. The laudable growth in interest in recent years and research projects such as SIR, MISLIP and INSIS[1] have focused attention on the need for pupils to handle information. Information technology is only valuable if seen in the light of improving pupils information skills because it is the ability of pupils to handle ideas and information which is at the heart of the educational process.

The advent of microcomputer use in school libraries has had a marked effect in both the use of school libraries by teachers and pupils and in their increasing relevance to teachers and pupils. New examination requirements such as GCSE emphasize the need for more individual work to be done by pupils, and teachers are now more aware that developing techniques involved in resource-based learning is vital in helping pupils to realise their true educational potential. School librarians have been active in promoting the use of the microcomputer *outside* the computer studies department and stressing the present and future need for pupils to be efficient in and aware of using information derived from microcomputers. The development of curriculum-related databases has meant closer cooperation between school librarians and teachers; greater use of a wider range of resources in the school library; and an improvement in pupils' ability to plan, organize and present projects and assignments to teachers.

The focus of this book is on school librarians and teachers working together and using the microcomputer for educational ends. The sharing of professional skills – the librarian's knowledge of database creation on the microcomputer and the organization and location of information in the school; and the teacher's knowledge of the curriculum and pupils' abilities – can allow a new freedom in schools to exploit new technology and make the curriculum more attractive and more interesting to pupils. Both teachers and librarians have a vested interest in allowing pupils to create their own sources of information and share them with other pupils as this encourages a wide range of educational and social skills. The effective use of the microcomputer can also lead to increased motivation among pupils who are now involved in the processes of learning through project planning sheets, developing search strategies prior to using the microcomputer, using prints-out to find information and then using keywords suggested by the print-out.

This book is designed to provide a guide to a number of important aspects of microcomputer use in schools. It offers a guide for the uninitiated school librarian or teacher wishing to learn the basics of microcomputer technology. Suggestions for techniques for acquiring a microcomputer for the school library – approaches to the school administration by school librarians *and* teachers – are included and can be used by school staff in preparing and supporting their own proposals. The variety of administrative uses of the microcomputer in the school library demonstrate how it can be used to save the valuable time of the school librarian and provide a tool which produces printed material of a professional quality. Uses of the microcomputer in word processing, as electronic blackboard or electronic newspaper or magazine are given to show the flexibility of much software which can be used by all members of the school community.

Database creation, the linking of information skills and information technology and the accessing of external databases, are all examples of how each school can make its microcomputers work towards fundamental educational aims and can use new technology to give pupils the opportunity to create and use information in a variety of ways. This is valuable in school, but it is also vital in the pupils' future careers, all of which will be affected by new technology and the need for information in various ways. After school, pupils will become adult consumers, employees, benefits claimants, houseowners, ratepayers and members of different groups in society. In all these aspects of their life, computerized information will be an everyday part of their lives and it is important that the use of the microcomputer in school is seen in the light of pupils' ability to use new technology to find and use information directly related to their own immediate purposes. School librarians and teachers have a responsibility to provide pupils with the appropriate skills and opportunities to use this technology.

The selection of software again identifies the need for school librarian-teacher cooperation as the selection has to be geared towards the needs of the curriculum and not biased towards attractive software packages which may be useful in the leisure environment of the home, but have little educational relevance. In-service training for school librarians in relation to microcomputer use in schools highlights all the above points and emphasizes the need for a coordinated approach to INSET for librarians and teachers.

The technology of tomorrow can be glimpsed at today and developments such as microcomputers 100 times more powerful than those in school today, the emergence of truly 'expert' systems, voice-activated microcomputers and a range of fifth generation 'thinking' microcomputers should excite rather than frighten school librarians and teachers.

The contributors to this book all emphasize that the starting point for using microcomputers in school libraries is the school curriculum and school librarians, teachers, student teachers and student librarians and all those involved in *information* technology in education, should use this book to develop their own knowledge of new technology and discover how the microcomputer can be used not for the sake of technology , but as a tool for learning.

References
1. SIR – Schools Information Retrieval Project
    MISLIP – Microcopmuter in the School Library Project
    INSIS – Information Skills in Schools Project

Chapter 1
An introduction to microcomputers
by James E Herring

This chapter is designed to answer a simple question – what do school librarians and teachers, with little or no experience of microcomputers, need to know in order to overcome the initial uncertainties which people have when faced with new technology? The chapter will cover hardware – the microcomputers; software – the programs needed to make computers work effectively; and it will provide an overview of possible applications of microcomputers for librarians and teachers working together in schools. Some of the applications will be examined in more detail in subsequent chapters.

The aim will be to provide the school librarian or teacher with the basic terminology needed to use and, importantly, to discuss the uses of microcomputers in the school library and in the classroom. The terminology may seem strange, as all terminology does, but it is worthwhile remembering that driving a car or operating a stereo system also involves the use of terminology, which we take for granted. The reasons for introducing terminology are that it will provide the reader

a) with confidence in using the microcomputer;
b) with the knowledge to discuss the various uses of the microcomputer with colleagues;
c) a basic knowledge of the microcomputer from which the reader can go on to discover other, more intricate aspects of the microcomputer.

Hardware
There are three main types of computers – mainframes, minicomputers and microcomputers. The main difference between the three types is size, both physical and in the size of the memory (see below). A *mainframe* computer can control the computing applications of a whole company or university. It costs thousands of pounds (a recent acquisition of a mainframe computer by a polytechnic cost £300,000) and it needs dedicated professional staff to operate and maintain it. A *minicomputer* can often carry out many of the tasks of a mainframe computer but is smaller and needs less staff. Because of developments in computer technology,

1

minicomputers are now able to do what mainframes did 10–15 years ago. Few schools will be able to afford minicomputers as the cost can be £10,000 + . The *microcomputer* is the result of further breakthroughs in computer design and the most advanced microcomputers, some costing under £2,000, can now perform as well as some minicomputers. Microcomputers are now common in homes as well as in schools and one uncomfortable fact facing school librarians and teachers is that pupils have a much greater *technical* knowledge of microcomputers than they have. In order to maintain the authority of the teacher or librarian and to make pupils aware that microcomputers do not exist merely for playing games but have a wider range of educational applications, it is important for the librarian or teacher to have basic knowledge of microcomputers.

Types of microcomputer
Microcomputers range in price and in quality from £100 to £3000. At the lower end of the market are 'home' computers which are designed often for computer enthusiasts for programming or for children or adults to play computer games. These include the Sinclair Spectrum, the Commodore VIC 20 and the Acorn Electron. In schools, 'home' computers are also used. Many UK primary and secondary schools have a Sinclair Spectrum. The most common microcomputer used in UK schools is now the BBC microcomputer range. Other types used include the Apple 2 and Apple 2e and the RML 380Z. In the USA, the educational market is dominated by Apple while in Australia, Apple and BBC microcomputers are used. Newer and more sophisticated microcomputers now on the market have been produced by IBM e.g. the IBM PC, Atari and Ferranti. Each year, new machines are produced which either have more functions or can carry out existing functions in a quicker and cheaper fashion. This means that any microcomputer used in a school will, in strict terms, be obsolescent, in that a new model will soon be available. However, if the microcomputer which the school has does what the school librarian and teachers desire, then the availability of other models need not be a worry. It is useful to know what other models can do since microcomputers have a limited life and it may be that in five years time, the librarian and teachers will be involved in seeking a replacement for the existing microcomputer. In this case, having a working knowledge of the types of microcomputer available will be important.

Parts of a microcomputer
A microcomputer, or more accurately, a microcomputer system (the microcomputer itself is like a car engine and without the rest of the

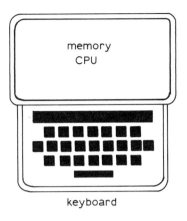

keyboard

Fig. 1.1

car, it cannot function effectively) consists of several parts. The **microcomputer** which is usually recognized as the part with the keyboard on top is the workhorse of the system. When the school librarian or the teacher uses the microcomputer, information (e.g. a list of books, a syllabus outline) will be keyed into the microcomputer via the keyboard, which is the same as an ordinary typewriter. The keyboard is the **input** device. This information is then processed by the **CPU** (Central Processing Unit). The CPU carries out certain operations with the information, but most importantly, it sends the information to the computer's **memory** (see Figures 1.1 and 1.2). The memory can store information which is put in, so that this information can be used again and it can hold a set of instructions for the computer to carry out. Once the information or instructions are put into the microcomputer, the user will want to check (a) what has been put in or (b) what the microcomputer can do with this information. Thus an **output** device is needed to make the user aware of what the microcomputer has done. The output will take the form of a monitor, or in some cases an ordinary television set. This device is also often referred to as a **VDU** (Visual Display Unit) (see Figure 1.3).

In simple terms, if the user typed in a list of books on a typewriter, s/he would be able to see what had been typed but could not do any more with this typed information apart from copying it. If the user wanted the list in alphabetical order, it would have to be retyped. Using the microcomputer, the school librarian could key in information of this type and the information would be sent by the CPU to the microcomputer's memory. If the librarian wanted the microcomputer to SORT the list by author, the microcomputer

3

would need some instructions on how to do this. This type of function is normally done by a **program.** A program is a list of instructions for the computer and when the program is **loaded** into the microcomputer, the CPU carries out each instruction until the task is complete. Thus the list would be **saved** in the computer's

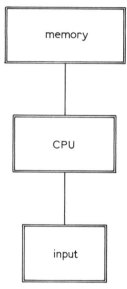

Fig. 1.2

computer

Fig. 1.3

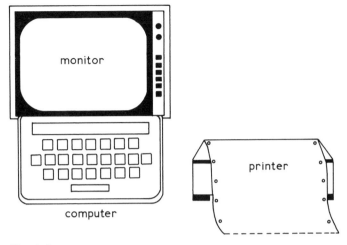

Fig. 1.4

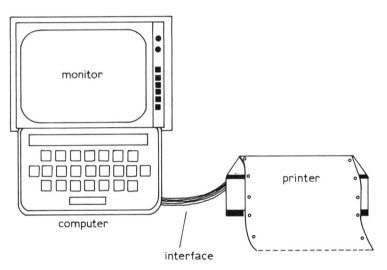

interface

Fig. 1.5

memory in alphabetical order and the school librarian could see the sorted list on the monitor. The other main output device is a **printer** (see Figure 1.4) which is linked to the microcomputer by an **interface** (see Figure 1.5). By using the printer, the librarian could produce one or more copies of the booklist, sorted by author or perhaps title. The information would remain in the computer's memory and copies taken at any time. Obviously, this cannot be done with a conventional typewriter.

To enable the user to make more effective use of the microcomputer, a device is needed for putting programs into the microcomputer quickly. A program can consist of thousands of instructions and to obviate the need for each program to be loaded separately, most microcomputers use a **mass storage device** or an **auxiliary storage device.** In most home computers, this device is a cassette tape recorder which relays the program from the tape into the computer's memory. In schools, most microcomputers now have **disk drives** which allow programs to be loaded in via **floppy disks** (see Figures 1.6 and 1.7).

A floppy disk is not unlike an LP record. It will contain a program or programs to allow the computer to be used in certain ways. For

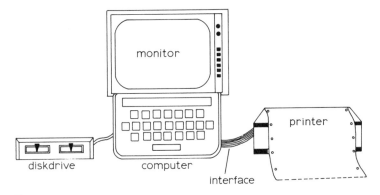

Fig. 1.6

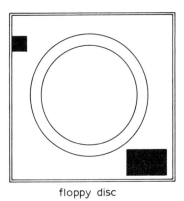

floppy disc

Fig. 1.7

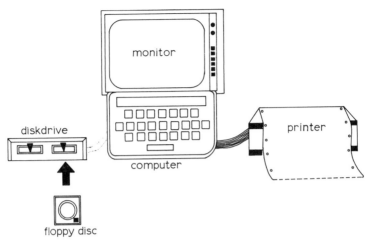

monitor

diskdrive

printer

computer

floppy disc

Fig. 1.8

example, programs exist which allow the microcomputer to act as an **on-line catalogue.** That is, instead of using the card catalogue, the pupils could use the microcomputer in the school library to search for information on a particular topic. The school librarian or teacher would use the programs on disk to create a list of references and the pupils would be able to use the microcomputer in the same way as they use a subject index. Once a disk is put into the disk drive (see Figure 1.8), a command is typed in on the keyboard, the microcomputer takes a copy of a particular program from the disk and puts it into its memory. The program is then activated by commands input by the pupil, teacher or librarian.

Once the school librarian or teacher has mastered the simple stages of switching on the different parts of the microcomputer, e.g. to set up the BBC microcomputer, the user

1) Plugs in the computer, the disk drive, the monitor and the printer
2) Switches on the microcomputer, the disk drive, the monitor and the printer
3) Puts a disk into the disk drive
4) Types in a command on the microcomputer

s/he will be able to use programs for different applications such as database creation or word processing and the applications are covered later in this book.

Apart from the above stages and terminology, there are some basic facts to be known which will enhance the user's understanding of the microcomputer and appreciate not only its uses, but very importantly, its limitations.

In terms of memory, the microcomputer has two types, known as **ROM** (Read only memory) and **RAM** (Random access memory). ROM consists of information the microcomputer needs to operate and run programs and many functions can be stored in ROM. A microcomputer can have ROM **microchips** for particular purposes. Thus a word processing package may be stored in ROM and accessed not by using a floppy disk but by giving the microcomputer a command, e.g. the BBC-B's WORDWISE package is accessed by typing in ★ W. and pressing the **return** key.

RAM does not hold any permanent information but receives, holds or deletes information as the user wishes. Thus the list of books mentioned in the example above, could be keyed in and sorted in RAM but if the microcomputer was switched off, the information would disappear as the RAM would be cleared. In order to keep the sorted list, the school librarian or teacher would have to ask the computer to **save** it on disk i.e. copy it on to the floppy disk.

The amount of RAM which a microcomputer has is vital. Most microcomputers used in schools have limited RAM sizes. The memory is measured in **bytes.** A byte is a computer term which is equal to one character. A typical microcomputer will have 48K or 64K of memory i.e. 48 or 64 Kilobytes or 48,000 bytes. What this means is that the memory will only hold 48,000 characters and this is shared between RAM and ROM. In practical terms, it means that a 48K microcomputer using floppy disks will only be able to handle a **database** (a computerized list of references or information) of *c.*400 records. It can be seen immediately that, in library terms, the 48K microcomputer could not replace the library catalogue. Newer models of microcomputer have much larger memories and the *Guardian* reported that Atari have a microcomputer, the Atari 11040ST which has 1MB (one million bytes) of memory as standard[1].

In order to use all this memory, to store large pieces of text or large amounts of data for pupils to work with, the newer computers will have to use **hard disk** facilities. A hard disk enables the microcomputer to store vast amounts of information on disk. Instead of the 400 records noted above on a floppy disk, a hard disk would enable the school librarian to enter 20,000 records i.e. to have the whole school library on disk, plus a record of materials in departments on disk also. The pupils would then have access to an **OPAC** (On-line public access catalogue) similar to those available in some polytechnics and universities at present.

One aspect of microcomputers which users find frustrating is that if the school librarian or teacher has access to only one type of microcomputer e.g. a BBC-B or an IBM PC, there is no **compatibility** between the machines.[2] If a record or cassette is bought in a shop, it will play on any type of stereo equipment, be it Amstrad, Sanyo, Phillips etc. Unfortunately, each make of microcomputer is designed differently and a program written for the BBC-B will not work on an IBM PC or an Apple 2e. A move to partly remedy this situation is the production of IBM compatible microcomputers. This means that several large microcomputer companies are designing computers which will run most IBM software and it may be that in ten years time, the problem of incompatibility will be lessened.

Other aspects of microcomputer use will involve linking microcomputers within one school or linking a school microcomputer to an external source of information. In many schools, computer rooms have a number of microcomputers linked into a **network**. This allows a number of pupils to work on different microcomputers but to link these microcomputers to a central microcomputer on which the program being used is stored. Thus a history class working on census data could access the data on a number of different microcomputers without the program or the data being copied for each microcomputer. Wider networks in schools are likely to be possible in the future. For example, if the school library's catalogue is on-line, it will be possible for pupils to search for information *from the classroom*. In this way, planning searches and integrating the microcomputer search stage of the information skills process (see Chapter 6) may be done in the classroom.

To access external sources of information, such as PRESTEL or TTNS or an on-line database such as DIALOG, the microcomputer will have to be linked to a **modem**. The modem can be connected to the telephone line and provide a link to such external sources.

Selecting a microcomputer
Because the range of microcomputers available changes so rapidly, choosing the 'right' microcomputer for a school library is an impossible task. In practical terms, the school librarian or teacher may not have the authority to make a final decision on the purchase of a microcomputer, but it is important that s/he has some knowledge of what microcomputers can do and what criteria should be used for selection, so that the decision made by the headteacher may be influenced by the person who will ultimately control and use the microcomputer.

Cost may be seen as the ultimate control in choosing a microcomputer and certain ranges of microcomputer e.g. hard disk units may be out of reach given the budget of an individual school or school library although the new Amstrad PC1512 offers a 20mb hard disk for under £1,000. Initially, selection should be based on needs and objectives. Asking questions such as – what can a particular microcomputer provide in terms of information retrieval or CAL or word processing, can provide the basis for choice. In some cases, authorities will have policies on the selection of microcomputers e.g. that all new microcomputers must be in the BBC range or be IBM compatible. There still remains the decisions on what is best value for money.

Selection will be primarily influenced by the availability of **software** i.e. the programs needed to operate the microcomputer e.g. if a microcomputer has an information retrieval program which is fast, reliable, user friendly *but* can only retrieve items by searching under one term i.e. a book or slide set on SPACE can only be found by entering the keyword MOON or the keyword STARS but the pupils cannot combine keywords and search for all items under MOON *and* PLANETS, then this program and this machine does not meet the needs of the school.

Selection is a question of balance. No one microcomputer will do all functions well. Some have excellent word processing programs but a poor range of CAL software. The librarian and the teachers will have to set priorities for information use and these priorities are likely to include

1) The availability of a flexible, easy to use information retrieval system, often called a **database management system** (DBMS) which will allow the creation of a very large database (e.g. OPAC) or smaller curriculum-related databases (see Chapter 5).

2) The availability of software, either on disk or on ROM chip, for facilities such as CAL, word processing and linking to external sources of information.

3) Room for expansion of the microcomputer i.e. can the RAM be extended by adding extra memory? Can a hard disk be added? Can different types of printer e.g. a letter quality printer be added?

4) What back-up in terms of advice and maintenance is available e.g. if the microcomputer breaks down, can it be attended to locally or will there be a delay? Is there a maintenance contract? In terms of advice, what future plans does the company have for this particular model i.e. a school does not wish to buy a microcomputer which will not be compatible with the next range of microcomputers produced by that company.

5) What is the *actual* cost of the microcomputer *system* i.e. the total cost of the microcomputer, the monitor, the disk drive, the printer, interfaces, add-on memory, modem plus software, printer paper and printer ribbons? Is there an educational discount?

6) Once the microcomputer has been purchased, is there a means of securing it? This is particularly important in schools where the microcomputers used e.g. the BBC-B, have a ready market for home use and are therefore vulnerable to theft. The microcomputer should have a form of security e.g. by bolting it to a desk if it is to remain in one place all the time, perhaps next to the library catalogue.

How to find out about microcomputers

The decision to purchase a microcomputer or to give advice on the purchase means that the school librarian and teachers will have to gather information in relation to the questions posed above on criteria for selection. The sources of information include other schools, colleges of education and schools of librarianship and information studies, the microcomputer manufacturers and printed sources.

Despite the dramatic revelations of new, super-microcomputers in the national and computer press, a school is likely to want to buy a microcomputer which is a known brand and which will suit the information needs of staff and pupils. One way of ensuring that a particular type of microcomputer is suitable, is to visit other schools, or school library services or teachers' centres to find out whether a particular microcomputer will be suitable in the individual school. It will be useful, for example, for the school librarian to visit other schools and discuss the uses of the microcomputer and ask questions about its range of software; its suitability e.g. do *teachers* and pupils use it?; its ability to cope with heavy use; its reliability as a system – does it break down? Is the quality of the printer good? Other questions on the potential use of the microcomputer such as the links with information skills in project work or database creation by pupils can also be asked. Crucially, a visit will allow the librarian or teacher to try the microcomputer out and see practical demonstrations.

A second source of information is to be found in schools of librarianship and information studies and in colleges of education. Such institutions should be able to offer advice and information on hardware, software, the use of microcomputers and also access to written sources of information in the form of books and periodical articles. In the School of Librarianship and Information Studies in RGIT, students doing projects on school libraries have worked with school librarians and teachers in creating databases for schools. This provides the school librarian and teacher with access to expertise, suitable software and can be a useful way of gaining firsthand experience of using a microcomputer. All colleges of education have computer departments who actually seek close cooperation with schools in developing computer use. Working with institutions of higher education can also be useful as a means of setting up a project to justify the use of the microcomputer in the school library (see Chapter 2).

Manufacturers of microcomputers such as Apple, Acorn, IBM, Amstrad and Atari will provide school librarians and teachers with information on their microcomputers and on the software available for them. Obviously, this source of information needs to be examined carefully as each manufacturer is attempting to sell its own particular product. By asking some of the questions listed above in the section on criteria, it is possible to compare the different systems. One temptation to be resisted is the special offer microcomputer which, despite its low price, may be the last in a series from that manufacturer and the user may find that no *new* software is being written for that model.

In terms of software, a general rule is that new computers will run most of the old software but that new software, written for updated versions of existing microcomputers is often incompatible with earlier versions. While it is not possible to be completely up to date, the user should not buy models with in-built obsolescence.

Printed sources will allow librarians and teachers to keep up with developments in the use of microcomputers in general and in particular uses in schools. In the library and information world, journals such as *Small Computers in Libraries*, *Program*, *Vine* and *Library Micromation News* all print articles on microcomputer use. For school librarians, *SLG News*, the *School Librarian*, *Education Libraries Bulletin*, *School Library Journal*, *Emergency Librarian* and *Australian School Librarian* provide up to date information on practice and research. In education, the *Times Educational Supplement* has occasional articles on microcomputers in schools, including school library use[3] as well as software reviews. More specifically dedicated to microcomputers are *Educational Computing*,[4] *Acorn User*, *Apple User*, *Journal of Computer Aided Learning*, *CET News*, *SCET News* and *Computer Education*. Useful advice for school librarians is also included in 'Getting started with micros'[5] a booklet produced for ILEA school and college librarians and in Costa and Costa's *A micro handbook*.[6]

Costs

The cost of the microcomputer system will vary according to the type of machine, size of memory, whether floppy or hard disks are used; the quality of printer and monitor bought and the cost of software used on the microcomputer. In UK schools, the BBC-B microcomputer is at present the most popular model used and such a system, including microcomputer, dual disk drive, monitor and printer will cost around £1300. While other microcomputers are cheaper than the BBC range, at present they do not have the range of software available to meet school needs. With rising competition, however, it may be that school librarians and teachers will choose to spend money on newer 16 **bit** (see Glossary) machines which will provide larger memories and a reasonable range of software in terms of database management packages, while continuing to use BBC microcomputers for CAL use in the library and in the classroom. Software costs can be quite low and information retrieval systems such as KWIRS, SIR, QUEST or MODIFIABLE DATABASE (see software list, Appendix 1) are available for around £20. In many cases, database management systems will be provided with the microcomputer although this would have to be judged in terms of suitability for use by pupils.

Microcomputer applications

The main thrust of this book is the *educational* use of microcomputers by school librarians and teachers in relation to the use of library and classroom resources. Microcomputers also have administrative uses and can prove useful in providing better management information for school librarians; in keeping records of stock orders and acquisitions; in providing letters, lists, handouts, plans and reports of high quality in production terms; in allowing school librarians to publicize their services and give pupils access to electronic noticeboards. These applications will be covered fully in Chapters 3 and 4 and can be seen as widening the range and scope of the school librarian's tasks and in providing an up to date technological approach to school library management which can only serve to improve the status of the school librarian and further teacher/librarian cooperation.

As will be shown below, the use of microcomputers to allow pupils to retrieve information sources for curricular work and viewing microcomputer use as an information skill which all pupils should acquire, ensures that the microcomputer is seen as a tool to enhance the learning done by pupils in schools. There is a danger of seeing new technology as an end in itself and of teaching pupils the mechanics of microcomputer use without looking at what is done before and after pupils use the microcomputer. Chapters 5 and 6 will demonstrate how the microcomputer can be used as part of the curricular work done by pupils and how it can greatly increase the use of school resources in the library and in the classroom. The fusion of school librarian and teacher skills will again be demonstrated.

As well as providing pupils access to information in the school, microcomputers have greatly widened the amount of information available to pupils by allowing access to external sources of data. Chapter 7 shows how the 'stock' of a school library can be added to via access to Prestel and how use of Prestel in turn increases the use of resources in the school. Information is no longer institution based and electronic sources of information such as Prestel and TTNS[7] provide school librarians and teachers with the opportunity to increase individual learning by pupils.

The school library has always been seen as a source of information and resources for pupils and teachers. With the advent of microcomputers in schools, computer software packages for CAL are being used in greater numbers by teachers and individual pupils. Chapter 8 examines the selection, acquisition and organization of computer software in school libraries and shows how the traditional working together by school librarians and teachers can be harnessed to these new sources of information and learning.

In-service training (INSET) is regarded as vital by all those employed in schools. INSET allows librarians and teachers to examine new approaches, to improve personal skills, increase productivity and keep up to date with new technological developments. Chapter 9 will provide a guide for INSET for school librarians with an emphasis on learning how to use microcomputers but particularly on the curricular implications of the use of microcomputers.

Future developments in the use of microcomputers including applications such as the use of expert systems, compact and video disks, electronic publishing and interactive video will be discussed in Chapter 10 and allow those starting to use microcomputers in schools to have a wider view of potential applications.

References

1. *Computer Guardian* 30/1/86.
2. For a list of IBM compatible microcomputers, see *Practical Computing*, 8,(7), July 1985, 81–3.
3. Malley, I., 'Complementary definitions', *Times Educational Supplement* 21.6.85, 65–6.
4. See for example Askey, J., 'This isn't work, it's fun', *Educational Computing*, July/August 1985, 14–15.
5. *Getting started with micros: a practical guide for school and college librarians*, ILEA, Learning Resources Branch, 1983.
6. Costa, B. and Costa, M., *A micro handbook for small libraries and media centres*, Libraries Unlimited, 1983.
7. For further information on TTNS, contact Times Network Systems Ltd, 200 Grays Inn Rd, London WC1X 8EZ.

Chapter 2
Justifying the microcomputer
by James E Herring

The main aim of this chapter is to provide guidelines for the introduction of a microcomputer into the school library or the extension of microcomputer work involving microcomputers in the school library and in the classroom. While each school will be different in terms of decision-making on computer and financial matters and different committees will exist, the mechanisms for acquiring a microcomputer and justifying its acquisition in educational terms, will be similar in all schools. The basic tool is likely to be a report to a headteacher or to a school committee and this chapter will attempt to suggest possible approaches to writing such a report, the prerequisites for the compilation of the report, who should write the report and the possible content of such a report. Examples from schools who have acquired microcomputers for their libraries will be used as sources of inspiration rather than documents to be copied verbatim.

It is worthwhile to look at what a report should achieve before discussing its content. Pat Booth's useful *Report writing*[1] states that certain decisions have to be made in writing a report, including

a) the *purpose* for which it is being written
b) the specific *topic*
c) the precise *message* to be delivered
d) the appropriate *structure*
e) suitable *length* and *format*
f) the right *vocabulary*, *style* and *tone*
g) the amount and kind of supporting *evidence* and *data.*

The purpose of this report will be firstly to demonstrate an interest in the educational use of the microcomputer in the school library on the part of the school librarian and others. This is important as it is unlikely that the headteacher or other teachers will have much knowledge of this topic. The use of the microcomputer for information retrieval and information use in schools has been neglected as a review of books on microcomputers in schools will show. The emphasis in schools has been on computer science and CAL. The report will therefore try to widen the knowledge of the school's decision-makers.

Secondly, the report should be seen as a means of persuading the school's hierarchy to devote resources to the school library but in the context of the microcomputer as a curricular tool. The purpose will be to emphasize the benefits to the whole school and not just to those normally associated with library use.

Thirdly, the report will be attempting to introduce new approaches to existing curricular work, with implications for the use of resources in the library and in the classroom, for teaching methods presently used in the school and for the skills pupils will use before, during and after they use the microcomputer i.e. information skills. If this is one of the purposes of the report, it will have to be handled diplomatically, if the report is not to be seen as too controversial.

What the report should try to do is to appear to offer an improvement in existing facilities and support to teachers and pupils without calling for a dramatic reorganization of timetables, syllabi or teaching methods.

Prerequisites

Before writing the report, the school librarian will have to consider certain factors involved in its compilation and also the consequences of submitting such a report. One consequence will be that the school librarian (and possibily teachers involved) will have to answer questions on the content of the report. An important prerequisite here concerns terminology. The report will outline what the microcomputer is to be used for and which microcomputer hardware and software will be needed. A knowledge of the terminology listed in Chapter 1 should cover these points. The librarian will have to anticipate questions on: the efficiency of the software; the capacity of the software and the microcomputer e.g. how many records can be handled by the software and what limitations will be created by the memory size of the microcomputer. If an information retrieval program is being used, it is likely that a printer will be needed and some knowledge of what type and quality of printer to be used will be required.

An important factor here will be the school librarian's experience of using the hardware and software. Thus before submitting the report, the librarian should be able to see the software demonstrated, perhaps at an in-service training day; to use the software either at the school library service HQ or by borrowing (but not copying) the software for use in the school. Because the school library does not have a microcomputer, the school librarian will have to gain access to one to use the software. Given the increasing numbers of microcomputers in schools and the fact that school librarians are generally in school after the school day ends, this should not prove problematic.

Experience in using microcomputers can also be gained through visits to other schools where microcomputers are already being used by school librarians and teachers in the school library. The benefits to be derived here are that the school librarian will be able to use the microcomputer with someone who has experience in another school. This will help as the experienced school librarian will already have gone through the process of justifying and acquiring a microcomputer and can anticipate the types of questions which might be asked by senior staff in the school. The information gained from visiting another school can be used in answering questions not just on the technical aspects of microcomputer hardware and software, but its actual use – how it links with the information skills programme; what curricular areas have been involved in other schools; will the microcomputer cause any problems in terms of security or pupil discipline?; will the school librarian be involved in training teachers in the use of the microcomputer for information handling?

With experience gained in using the microcomputer both in and out of school, the school librarian should, before presenting the report, be confident enough in using the microcomputer to be able to demonstrate its uses and suggest potential uses to staff such as the school's Head of Resources. An important point here is that existing school staff may have little experience of using microcomputers for information retrieval and the school librarian needs to impress the staff by her/his ability in using the microcomputer.

Once suitable experience has been gained, the school librarian can develop a plan for the report. A vital element in the report will be a specific educational project, to be jointly managed by the school librarian and a teacher or teachers. The use of the microcomputer is to be shown to be directly related to the curriculum and to enhance pupils' learning, thus the project must be curriculum-based and not restricted to pupils' use of the library for general work. It should be made clear that the microcomputer is not to be used in a 'library project' created by the librarian solely to teach pupils how to use the library. The schools where successful use of the microcomputer in the library is evident, have all begun with small projects involving the librarian and one or two teachers.

The project should be discussed by the school librarian and the teachers to examine

a) what is being taught
b) what skills pupils are expected to acquire

c) what aspects of information handling are involved
d) at what stage of the project will pupils use the microcomputer
e) what information the pupils will gain from the microcomputer
  and how this information will be used

In Bridge of Don Academy in Aberdeen, a project was set up by the school librarian and the modern studies teacher who was teaching a class of third-year pupils on the topic of 'Conflict and the protection of the environment'. The discussion between the teacher and the school librarian covered the content of the course being done by pupils, in this case aspects of pollution in cities, in the countryside and in the sea. The skills aspect a project should cover include the skills acquired in the classroom, such as the ability to identify different types of pollution or the causes of pollution. Skills in handling information in both the classroom and the library – the definition of purpose, finding information and using information – should also be discussed. Thus 'information handling' does not merely cover using the microcomputer to find references to aspects of pollution such as ACID RAIN but to the whole process of learning done in the classroom and the school library.

The school librarian and the teachers need to discuss the use of the microcomputer in the library, in particular the stage of the course when the library will be used. This will depend on how much work the pupils have to do in class before using the library. For example, the pupils may learn about the principles of environmental control in class before going on to complete an assignment on some aspect of pollution, as happened in Bridge of Don Academy. The school librarian and teacher will then decide on what resources are available in terms of books, non-book materials, periodical articles etc. and how these could be used as the basis for creating a curriculum-related database (see Chapter 5).

The justification for acquiring a microcomputer will lay stress on educational benefits and the school librarian and teachers will plan how the pupils will use the information they obtain from the microcomputer as a step in the learning process. This will include how pupils will use their keyword searches in finding information from the microcomputer and then how they use these keywords when they follow up references to books and other materials. Skills such as skimming, scanning and note taking are important here and it will be useful in planning the project and in the report, if these information skills are clearly linked to the use of the microcomputer.

There also needs to be a plan for evaluating the project and the librarian and the teacher should discuss the evaluation of the pupils' ability to use the microcomputer (technical skills) and their ability to make use of the information they gain from the microcomputer (information skills). Evaluation of the project can also be seen in terms of how useful the teacher sees the microcomputer in the project. For example, in the MISLIP project teachers in different subjects (biology, history, English) found that the microcomputer helped pupils to plan projects better and improved the motivation of pupils; while the school librarian at Bankhead Academy pointed to the use of a wider range of resources by pupils in the school library.

The benefits of planning such a project are that, by outlining the project in a report, the school librarian is demonstrating the educational use of the microcomputer but is doing so in terms of the use of the microcomputer by the school librarian *and* a subject teacher or teachers. In effect, the report is stemming not just from the librarian and does not only concern the library. A curriculum-based report is likely to have a greater chance of success because it shows benefits to pupils, the teachers and the school librarian i.e. the whole school. It is important that the school library's microcomputer will be seen as a whole-school resource and not just as a mechanical tool for improving the efficiency of the school library.

The school librarians who have acquired microcomputers have either produced reports on particular projects and gained part-time access to a microcomputer for that project, but have subsequently been given a microcomputer permanently in the library or, as in the case of St Modan's High School (see Examples) have produced reports on the acquisition of a microcomputer for a range of purposes.

A 'model' report of the first approach might contain the following elements –

Title: Information technology, the school library and the curriculum

Project: The use of a library-based microcomputer and information retrieval system in 2nd year Integrated Studies

Staff: M. Wright (School Librarian), J. West (History), F. Strong (Geography)

Aims: To link the development of pupils' information skills with information technology in the classroom and in the school library

Objectives:
1. To improve pupils' ability in planning project work
2. To introduce pupils to information retrieval using a micro-computer-based information retrieval system

19

3. To encourage pupils to make greater use of a wide range of curricular resources in the school library and in the classroom
4. To improve pupils' ability to use information effectively

Methodology:
Pupils in the 2nd-year Integrated Studies 'People and the environment' course will be given 'free choice' assignments in this curricular area. Each pupil will choose, under guidance of a teacher, a particular area of investigation. Planning sheets for identifying the purpose of the project will be used in class. Pupils will use resources in the S2 Resource Area and in the school library for their project. Part of the project will be a search done on the microcomputer in the school library. A curriculum related database, entitled 'Environment' will be created by the school librarian and teachers involved, using curriculum related keywords identified from the 'People and environment' course.

Pupils will be expected to use keywords in searching for information, in locating resources and in using resources. There will be an emphasis on the skills of identifying purpose, finding information, using information, including note making, the organization of information and the presentation of information, throughout the project. Pupils will submit print-outs of their searches on the microcomputer as part of their project presentations.

Hardware, software and materials:
Hardware   A BBC-B microcomputer with dual disk drive and printer will be required in the library for, at minimum, one day per week for the whole of term 2.
Software   The KWIRS package (or SIR or QUEST) will be available either on loan from the School Library Service or, preferably, the school may purchase the software (Cost £20).
Materials   Printer paper and a supply of floppy disks for database creation and use, will be required.

Timescale: The project will start in week 2 of Term 2 and finish in week 11.

Evaluation:
Both teachers and the school librarian will be monitoring pupils' responses to

1) information skills planning sheets
2) the keyword approach to identifying the purpose of, searching for and using information

3) using a microcomputer to search for information
4) worksheets on note taking, organizing and presenting information

A report on the project will be drawn up in Term 3.

M. Wright (School Librarian)
J. West (History Dept)
F. Strong (Geography Dept)

Such a report obviously does not guarantee success and both school librarians and teachers involved in projects such as this are well aware of the need to be fully cognizant with school politics in seeking to use resources. For example, it might be very useful to get verbal agreement, in principle, from the head of computing studies for the release of a microcomputer for the duration of the project. Also, it may be politic to tell the deputy head or head of resources to whom the project proposal will be presented, that the proposal is in progress, so that the ground is prepared. Each school will have to identify the best means of and route for communication but this is something which school librarians in particular, being outside the subject departmental structure, learn about very quickly.

Once the project has been carried out and shown to be successful, subsequent written or verbal reports can outline other uses of the microcomputer based in the school library, leading to the acquisition of a library based microcomputer or the reallocation of an existing microcomputer to the school library.

There will be many reasons put forward why the school library *cannot* have its own microcomputer but it is up to the school librarian and interested teachers to present a reasonable case, based firmly on educational grounds. The 'golden rules' for such an approach might be summed up as

Do not work alone
Argue the case on educational grounds
Present a professional report

Examples
The following are examples from schools where at least one microcomputer is now permanently based in the school library. As can be seen they are the work of school librarians and teachers working in partnership. The St Modan's High School proposal covers a range of uses for the microcomputer, while the Dyce

21

Academy proposal is for a specific project. The Dyce project was based (with permission) on the Houghton Regis project (see Chapter 9) and contains the original proposal and part of an evaluation report which is being prepared. The Wandsworth School example shows a document used by the librarian at the school's Computer Committee.

St Modan's High School
Study Across the Curriculum
Project
Setting up of an Information Technology area within the library

Project aim
To allow pupils to became familiar with, and gain experience of present and future means of information retrieval

Project objectives
1. By use of the computer's appeal to pupils
   a) promote an attitude of inquiry
   b) encourage an awareness of the process of inquiry skills
2. Enhance study skills in preparation for tertiary education
3. Train pupils in methods of information retrieval
4. Allow pupils in group or personal study to take advantage of national databanks and broaden the scope of their study
5. Promote an awareness of present and future trends in Information Technology

Objective 1
This would be aimed mainly at the 12-14 age group although the middle and upper schools could participate to a lesser extent.

Instruction would be given by the librarian and the class teacher and it would deal mainly in concrete activities rather than abstract theory and should be tied to specific project work.

Different methods of information retrieval would be taught.
   a) conventional e.g. card index
   b) electronic e.g. databases
The use of keyboards would be emphasized.

Pupils would then be encouraged to practise and develop these skills in their own projects.

Because these skills would not be particular to one subject area – but rather should be seen as an integral part of the whole schooling process – the project should have a cross-curricular base, be taught within subject areas in reference to specific contexts rather than as a separate theoretical concept related to general study. The student once having obtained these skills would then be encouraged to extrapolate these in the wider area of general study.

Objective 2
This would be the extension of inquiry skills into the middle and upper schools. It would be aimed not only at those intending to continue to tertiary education but to all pupils.
Two pronged approach

1. Tuition in study skills and information retrieval methods especially electronic. This to be provided by librarian and teacher.
2. CM RBL in study skills and subject areas. This will require the development of CAL material in study skills and the purchase of CAL programs in subject areas which will be held as a library resource.

Objective 3
Information retrieval should be recognized as a skill within its own right, though it forms an integral part of wider study skills.

The increasingly complex organization of information within our society demands that training be given to all members of the school population, as opposed to simply those destined for tertiary education, in information retrieval skills.

The success of Objectives 1 and 2 is based on a thorough acquisition of information retrieval skills and a recognition of their interdependence. Information skills would be taught in a structured, integrated and progressive manner as outlined in Objectives 1 and 2.

Objective 4
More and more departments using RBL as a method of instruction may see personal or group projects as a valid and worthwhile means of extension study on a personal level.

Access to national and local databases would greatly enhance the potential and validity of these projects by giving a greater selection of resources, variety of materials and methods of organization.

Objective 5
Information technology is now an integral part of everyday life. It can be argued that it is the responsibility of the school to develop this essential life skill. It might be held that the place for this would be in the Computer Studies Curriculum but to do this would preclude a large number of pupils from acquiring basic handling skills.

It should be regarded as life and leisure (SOC & VOC) rather than 'school'. Familiarity can be learned with the minimum of instruction and easily obtained simply by practice.

It follows therefore that it should be cross-curricular and readily accessible to all, and therefore in the library.

Equipment
1. Small teletext receiver, preferably with remote control.
2. Microcomputer with subscription to national network and printer.
3. Wider area databases.
4. Computer Managed Learning (CML) areas with one or two micros DD and UDU.

The minimum requirements for this would be a television receiver equipped with teletext and microcomputer access to one of the national networks such as Prestel. It is recognized that this might cause expenditure problems in telephone expense but, if it is sited in the library, it is under constant supervision and control, which would preclude unauthorized use of the telephone system and allow a proper accounting system of telephone costs, which could be charged to the per capita of the department using the system, similar to the way in which Rank Xerox is administered.

Carol Stewart (School Librarian)
James Henderson (Asst Principal Teacher, Computer Studies)

Dyce Academy
Dyce Community Information Database (Dycetel)
Aims
1. To familiarize pupils with the skills of planning and organizing information.
2. To familiarize pupils with the creation and use of a database.
3. To familiarize pupils with the use of outside databases e.g. Prestel.
4. To gather and organize community information, both current and historical, using a variety of sources (including PRESTEL and information collected in the Domesday Project).
5. To produce a database using the COMMUNITEL system.
6. To make this database available to the community (long-term aim).
7. To familiarize pupils with the microcomputer and its uses.

Methodology
Initially a small database would be created as a pilot study. This database would be created by three S3 pupils from a General Studies class. They would be involved in planning the database, collecting the data, organizing the data and creating the database. During the early stages, the database would have information on defined areas of community information. In the later stages, the initial database would be expanded and updated.

Content of database in early stages
DYCE – basic information:
 – the area
 – transport (rail, air, bus, roads)
 – population
DYCE – Community Centre:
 – where
 – opening times
 – facilities
 – what's on
 – cost of using
 – who to contact

Employment and careers
– careers service (what it does, who to contact, when, where)
– firms who employ school leavers in Dyce
– YTS (what it is, where in Dyce, who to contact)
– Statistics from the area
– Unemployment (Aberdeen)

Information on the Community Centre would involve close work with the staff of the Community Centre. Information on careers would involve close work with the Careers Service and the Dyce Academy Careers Adviser.

Skills used by pupils in creating Dycetel (Local Community Information) Database
Planning
Discussion of task
Decide purpose of task
Discussion of time-scale
Creation of word web using existing knowledge

Identification of Possible Sources
Discussion of sources

25

Location of possible sources
Use of local library and school library
– use of alphabetical index
– use of subject index
– use of local community index

Use of telephone directory
– alphabetical skills

Use of local directory
– alphabetical skills

Contacting sources
Use of external database (Prestel)
– use of computer
– use of alphabetical index
– keyboard skills

Use of dictionary

Letter writing
– use of word processor
– use of computer
– keyboard skills

Use of telephone (verbal communication)

Use of street plan

Use of bus timetables

Questioning sources (done without anyone from school present)
Planning questions

Verbal communication
– introducing themselves
– explanation of task
– asking questions
– concluding discussion

Recording and storing information
Note taking

Organization of notes

Evaluation of information
Analysis of notes

Reappraisal of topic (discussed aims)

Rejection of unnecessary information

Presentation of communication
Appraisal of audience

Reappraisal of word web using information gathered

Organization of database
– decide on headings/subheadings
– sequence
– cross-referencing

Use of computer
– keyboard skills
– graphic skills
– use of Prestel
– language/presentation
– layout

Use of (COMMUNITEL) viewdata
– routing/cross referencing
– discussion of limitations/size

Final evaluation (Outline)
Evaluation of database re aims and objectives

Demonstration of database

Re-evaluation of database after use by others

Lynda M Bain (School Librarian)
Joan Sadler (Asst Head Teacher)

Wandsworth School
Computers are tools
1. Hands-on opportunity for staff. The microcomputer will be readily available in a non-specialist environment; seen in a place frequently visited for other purposes. Help will be available, discussion can be easily stimulated via the use of other media. Microcomputers are non-threatening.
2. Staff can become familiar with CAL programs before using them with students and can use word processing packages.
3. Pupils will be able to use the microcomputer for games, work and word processing (i.e. more 'hands-on' opportunities).
4. Information skills classes (run by the librarian) can include the

use of databases as part of normal search procedures and the creation of small specialist databases can be part of the course or can be made in advance for specific topics.

5. So that meaningful searches can be made on the microcomputer and so that all students will be familiar with its use, eventually all audiovisual items in the library will be entered on to a database. This is a long-term project, possibly not to be embarked upon until after 'reorganization' – if this is inevitable.

Similarly, amalgamated schools might well enter their subject indexes.

The main aim of all the above would be to ensure that using a microcomputer as a tool becomes as natural as using a telephone or a typewriter.

Margaret O'Shea (School Librarian)

Chapter 3
Administration, publicity and information
by James E Herring

This chapter will cover a variety of uses of the microcomputer in the school library involving the school librarian, teachers and pupils. There are a number of programs available for different types of microcomputer which allow school librarians to offer a range of services to their users and this chapter will cover computerized acquisition packages, word processing programs, microcomputer-based publicity packages, including electronic noticeboards and the use of the microcomputer by staff and pupils in producing quality output in terms of textual and graphic design of worksheets, information bulletins and school newspapers.

Acquisitions
Ordering and receipt of materials for the school library is not normally a large part of the school librarian's work but it can prove time-consuming and one advantage of having a microcomputer-based acquisitions package is that it will help to free the school librarian for other more curriculum-related work and will allow easy access to books and other items on order using a program which can be searched in various ways. Programs are available for different types of microcomputer including ORDERIT for the Apple 2 and 2e, and PROTOKOL for the BBC-B, which are specifically designed as acquisitions programs. School librarians can also use programs such as Dbase 2 which is a flexible database management package which can be used for acquisitions and other purposes. An acquisitions program should ideally indicate the author, title, publisher and date of an item on order, the date on which the order was sent and the name of the supplier of particular items. It should allow access by different fields, so that, for example, a teacher should be able to inquire whether a particular item has arrived in the library by identifying the author or the title of the item or by giving the name of the teacher who recommended its acquisition for the school library.

PROTOKOL is a menu driven acquisitions program for the BBC-B microcomputer. The user is given the option of entering a record or simply entering the bibliographic details and classification number of each item to be ordered. The second feature allows the user to search the records for any item by any of the bibliographic fields and the user can also obtain print-outs of listings of records under the various fields. PROTOKOL also has the facility to produce catalogue cards for each item. The system will produce an author card and title card for each item, then show the next item on screen with the option of printing. PROTOKOL comes in the form of a ROM chip and operates with a number of programs on a master disk which also contains datafiles.

ORDERIT for the Apple 2 microcomputer is also a very simple program. The user is given on screen a list of fields covering author, title, publisher, date and price. This record can then be printed and sent to the suppliers. When the item is received, the record is deleted from the file and the amended file can be printed out. An example from ORDERIT might read:

```
AUTHOR       :  COUPER, Heather
TITLE        :  EXPLORING SPACE
PUBLISHER    :  TREASURE PRESS
DATE         :  1984
PRICE        :  £5.99
```

More sophisticated (and more expensive) software such as Dbase 2, which is available for different microcomputers with CP/M (see Glossary) allows the user to create a number of fields of his/her own choosing and, in effect, to give more flexibility than programs such as PROTOKOL or ORDERIT. The advantage of systems such as Dbase 2 are that the user controls the number of fields available (e.g. the school librarian may wish to have a field for the person who ordered the item and a teacher could have a list of all books or items ordered by him/herself or by the Geography department) and the size of each field, which is limited by other programs. The librarian therefore has to choose between software which is readily and easily usable but which is inflexible and software which needs to be 'programmed' but which allows the user to tailor the software to the needs of one particular library.

Word Processing
Costa and Costa[1] argue that word processing programs on microcomputers 'have a way of transforming even computerphobes into dedicated believers of the "how did I ever live without it" variety' and, such is the difference in quality of output between documents produced on a word processor and those handwritten or typed on a conventional typewriter, that school librarians, teachers and pupils quickly become convinced of the need for and extensive uses of such programs.

A word processing package should allow the user to create documents which can be viewed on screen, saved on disk, loaded into the microcomputer's memory, amended on screen and printed out according to the format devised by the user.

Until recently, word processors were stand-alone machines costing thousands of pounds. The advent of microcomputers with word processing programs now means that the school librarian or teacher or pupil can have the facilities of the stand-alone word processor without the expense.

Most word processing programs, such as WORDWISE, VIEW, APPLEWRITER and EDWORD allow the user to work from a menu. The WORDWISE program will be used as an example here but the options are very similar in all packages and once the user learns the basics of word processing, switching between programs is relatively easy and it is likely that schools will have different types of word processing programs in the school library, in the computer room and in classrooms.

Using WORDWISE+,[2] the user is given the following menu:

WORDWISE-PLUS
© Computer Concepts 1984

1) Save entire text
2) Load new text
3) Save marked text
4) Load text to cursor
5) Search and replace
6) Print text
7) Preview text
8) Spool text
9) Segment menu
ESC Edit Mode
Please enter choice

To create a document, the user presses the ESCAPE key and is given a screen showing:

START
END

This is the equivalent of a blank page on which the user might write or type. The text of the document – a school librarian's information skills worksheet or a pupil's dissertation – can be keyed in via the microcomputer keyboard which is used in the same way as a typewriter. One aspect of word processing that the user has available in most programs is the facility to use FUNCTION KEYS on the keyboards (e.g. these keys are in red on the BBC microcomputer and run from f0 to f9). In WORDWISE+, if the user presses the f1 key and types in, at the beginning of the document

LM10 (this appears in green letters to distinguish it from the actual text)

then presses the f2 key, the user is instructing the program that s/he wishes to have a left hand margin of 10 spaces throughout the document. Thus by using the function keys f1 and f2, the user might type in the following:

(f1)LM10(f2) (f1)JO(f2) (f1)EP(f2)

On screen, the user would see, in green letters

LM10   JO   EP

This would result in a document which had a left hand margin of 10 spaces (LM10), was justified (JO) and was paginated (EP). At the bottom of each page, starting with PAGE 1, the word processing program would print out the appropriate page by adding 1 to the number on the previous page. Because of the limitations of memory on most microcomputers presently used in schools, each file is restricted to a certain number of pages. This can be overcome by creating and printing out several files in sequence and a command can be input which will instruct the program to continue pagination over several files. In WORDWISE+, the command

(f1)PN12(f2)

could be input for a file which the user wished to start at PAGE 12.

The major benefit of a word processing program is the flexibility it offers the user in amending documents. The user can quickly key in the document without having to take great care not to make mistakes in spelling or layout, as is necessary with a typewriter. When a draft of the document has been completed, the user can save the document on disk, e.g. by using option 1 on WORDWISE+, then printing the document out e.g. by choosing option 6 in WORDWISE+. Depending on personal preference, the user can scan the print-out for errors or amendments needed in wording or layout or, without printing the document, can view what has been written on screen. In

WORDWISE+, text can be viewed in large-scale lettering on screen as it is keyed in and the user can go through the text, using the arrow keys on the keyboard, making any necessary amendments. The vital key here is the **delete** key on the keyboard. Pupils often refer to this as the 'Tippex button' as it provides the user with an instant eraser of letters, words or phrases. Word processing programs allow the user to delete one character or word or sequence of words and insert new letters (e.g. to correct spelling) or new words or phrases to improve the clarity of the document. Once all amendments have been made, the amended document can be saved (e.g. by choosing option 1 in WORDWISE+) and the final version printed out.

For the school librarian and teacher, word processing programs on microcomputers allow the creation of documents which can be used once only e.g. a current new acquisitions list or a notice to pupils, but also documents which can be saved and used again. Library guides and information skills planning sheets are examples of documents which can be used with different classes and amended for use each new session. This obviously saves much time and effort as well as allowing for the creation of more imaginatively produced work.

For pupils, several advantages can be identified in the use of word processing programs. Stonier and Conlin[3] point out that, 'A word processor allows the student the opportunity of correcting their own work before presenting it to the teacher as a finished product'. The skills involved in drafting work, examining what has been written and *thinking* about what has been written in relation to the original *purpose* of the assignment are skills which teachers stress heavily. Word processing programs allow pupils to apply such skills in the creation and revision of their work.

Such programs have been used in a number of curricular areas. English teachers, for example, in both primary and secondary schools use word processing packages to allow pupils to create their own stories. In some cases, pupils are given the beginning or ending of a story and they have to complete the rest of the story in their own words. Working singly, or often in pairs, the programs allow for the development of a number of skills including social skills, such as cooperation, discussion (e.g. on content or amendments).

One major advantage to pupils and an important motivational factor in the use of word processing programs is that the pupils can obtain a print-out of their work. Papert[4] states that such facilities, '. . . can make a child's experience of writing more like that of a real writer'. As with pupil-created databases, word processing allows pupils to produce work which is professional in layout and which can be used by other pupils. There are few opportunities in school life for pupils to do this.

More senior pupils in schools can use a word processor to write up projects or dissertations for internal or external examinations. In St Modan's High School, senior pupils use the library's microcomputer and the WORDWISE program to complete dissertations. In one instance, a pupil's dissertation was 'lost' through an operating error but a number of pupils divided up the work, which was in final draft, took it to the computer room and keyed in the text in sections. A good example of cooperative skills being employed.

Some word processing packages have additional programs which can be used to check spelling errors or produce indexes. SPELLCHECK can be used with WORDWISE+ and VIEW and allows the user to have documents scanned for errors in spelling. Such programs have a dictionary disk and the spelling in the document is compared to that in the dictionary and corrected where necessary. SPELLCHECK has a dictionary of over 6000 words which can be related to text on file. While such programs are valuable for school librarians and teachers, in that most spelling errors are, in fact *typing* errors, they may be less useful for some pupils, as the act of checking for errors may be a way of improving their spelling, perhaps related to the use of dictionaries, and their use of language.

VIEWINDEX is an automatic indexing system designed to be used in conjunction with the VIEW word processing program. This gives the user the opportunity to produce an index to a long document such as a report or a dissertation. VIEWINDEX searches through the text held in VIEW files and collects words or phrases, which are selected by the user, to be included in the index. The index may be based on page numbers or in a report, in section order.

To use VIEWINDEX, the user prepares files of text using VIEW as a normal word processing program but certain words are highlighted for the index. An index file is then created on disk and this file gives a list of all the index entries and the page numbers or section numbers, as they are found. The system also contains a **sort** program which converts the index file into a completed text file in the order the user wishes – usually alphabetical order. The user can then edit the index if any entries need amending. A facility such as VIEWINDEX, while not an essential feature of a word processing package, nevertheless gives school users the opportunity to improve the quality of their reports. For pupils, the exercise of highlighting keywords or phrases can be a useful way of having pupils think more carefully about the structure and content of what they are writing.

Publicity
School librarians have traditionally publicized their services through displays, notices, flowcharts, library guides and, in user education

programmes, by means of tape-slide programmes and video recordings. The microcomputer now presents the school librarian with the opportunity to produce new types of publicity materials and information displays by using the microcomputer to produce electronic noticeboards, interactive library guides on screen and school magazines or newspapers either on screen or in hard copy. The software can also be used by pupils for curricular purposes.

Most pupils are now familiar with the teletext information pages on television's Ceefax and Oracle facilities and many schools now have access to Prestel (see Chapter 7). The EDFAX and COMMUNITEL packages are teletext emulators which allow school librarians, teachers and pupils to create, store and revise pages of information in a way similar to teletext. The use of COMMUNITEL as a package linked to the use of Prestel and the development of information skills is well documented in the Houghton Regis School project and has been used by Prestel Education as publicity material.[5]

The potential uses of such packages can be seen by examining the different ways in which school librarians and pupils can effectively present information in a novel and professional way. EDFAX, used by many schools in Bedfordshire, Lincolnshire, ILEA, Nottinghamshire and Grampian Region, will be used here as an example.

The EDFAX documentation[6] states that the program allows users to

- compose and edit *teletext* pages of information
- store pages of information on disk
- recall pages of information from disk and display them on a screen
- create a local electronic magazine, database or noticeboard
- develop artistic and creative skills relating to the presentation of information
- develop language and communication skills
- gain an understanding of the videotex display format.

School librarians using EDFAX will be involved with all the above skills in their roles as organizers and presenters of information to their users and as advisors and tutors to pupils in the skills of creating, organizing and using information. One obvious starting point for school librarians using the EDFAX program is in the creation of electronic noticeboards.

When using the EDFAX program to create pages of information, the school librarian will be presented with a menu of options:

Editing Menu
1) Create/Edit a page
2) Display a page
3) Display the directory
4) End the program
Select an option

When option 1 is selected, the user is shown a blank page on to which text and graphics can be entered. EDFAX has several attractive features to enhance the display of information, including five different colours for text and graphics or for background colour; double height lettering for emphasis; flashing text or graphics for more dramatic effect; and a variety of graphics, allowing the user to combine a variety of shapes, called pixels, to create pictures on screen. Pages of text and graphics can be designed in advance using the EDFAX Screen Planner which is included with the EDFAX package. This is a detailed grid representing the screen – rather like graph paper. (See p. 000).

One limiting factor about the EDFAX program is that the user does not have the facility to print out what has been created on screen. Any display or notice must be viewed on screen. For school librarians producing noticeboards with lists of new books, as done in Lossiemouth High School, it means that library users have to copy details down. The COMMUNITEL program has more advanced facilities than EDFAX, in that pages, created in a way very similar to that in EDFAX, can be printed out. Figure 3.1 shows an example of a print-out from COMMUNITEL. A further advantage of COMMUNITEL is that pages of information can be downloaded from Prestel and saved for further use with, for example, business studies or economics classes or the Prestel pages can be editied for school use. The school librarian can save the Prestel graphics on screen and add school information on to pages, thus saving much time in the creation of graphics.

Both EDFAX and COMMUNITEL programs can allow pupils to work creatively in the school library, producing their own noticeboards for school information on sports reports, school clubs and societies, lunch menus, social events in school, local pop concerts and other current information. In many schools, pupils use the programs as part of their curricular work in the handling of information and one of the bonuses to be derived from the use of teletext emulators is that there is no limit to the different curricular applications – constructing graphs in mathematics, maps in geography, diagrams in science or designs in art. Pupils are given the opportunity to use new technology in a creative way and enhance the

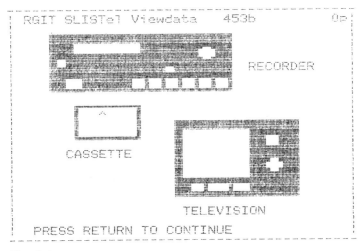

RGIT SLISTel Viewdata   45a   Op
    HOW TO USE THE A-V MATERIAL
    HOW TO USE THE A-V MATERIAL

PRESS 0 FOR SOUND CASSETTE
   " 1 FOR VIDEO CASSETTE
   " 2 FOR SLIDES
   " 3 FOR TAPE/SLIDE PACKAGES
   " 4 FOR MICRO-FICHE
   " 5 FOR COMPUTER SOFTWARE

IF AT ANY TIME YOU WISH TO RETURN TO
THIS MENU PRESS 0.

RGIT SLISTel Viewdata   453b   Op

                              RECORDER

CASSETTE

                    TELEVISION
PRESS RETURN TO CONTINUE

Fig. 3.1

quality of their own learning. EDFAX and COMMUNITEL can be
seen very much in the discovery learning sector of computer software
and school librarians and teachers can be instrumental in guiding
pupils to be creative, using a range of information and artistic skills.

The current revolution in the newspaper industry has highlighted
the growing use of new technology to produce daily newspapers.

Some of the facilities available to national newspapers are now available on programs for microcomputers and can be used by school librarians and teachers in schools. FLEET STREET EDITOR and AMX PAGEMAKER are two programs which allow the creation of school newssheets or newspapers.

FLEET STREET EDITOR allows users to produce quality printed material using a variety of graphics. The user works on a screen simulating an A4 page split into panels. The Graphics Library, provided with the package, contains a collection of illustrations, signs and typefaces which can be loaded from disk on to the page on which the user is working. Figure 3.2 shows examples from the Graphics Library.[7] The user can go through the Graphics Library and choose suitable graphics for his/her page. These graphics can then be enlarged or reduced and positioned anywhere on the page. The user can also cut out pieces from the graphics and add to the graphics in any form.

Once graphics have been loaded on to the Working Area, the Studio facility is then used. This allows the user to use a number of 'function icons' which are displayed at the side of the screen. By selecting different icons, the user can load panels of graphics from the disk, reduce or enlarge the graphics, use icons such as the 'Black frame icon' which draws a box round the graphic to highlight it, and use a variety of 'pens' for free hand drawing on the screen. The 'Copydesk' facility allows the user to input text in various forms on to the screen and thus create a true newspaper page. There are options for producing headlines, for using different typefaces and for positioning text on the screen. Text is input as if the user was using a word processing program and files from VIEW or WORDWISE can be incorporated. The 'Page make-up' facility is where the screen is split into different panels and the user can make final decisions on the layout of the text and graphics. The program then allows the user to preview what has been created before the page is finally printed out.

FLEET STREET EDITOR and AMX PAGEMAKER are two programs with a variety of uses in school. The school librarian can produce a library bulletin or newspaper in an attractive format and pupils can be encouraged to use the library as an information base in the truest sense – where information about the school is gathered, classified and presented back to the school in a readable and attractive form. For teachers, such programs allow for, as in word processing programs, the development of a range of educational skills. Many English teachers already have newspaper projects in which pupils produce articles and stories on paper. Using microcomputer programs to produce 'real' newspapers can only add to the motivation of pupils as well as to the quality of the final

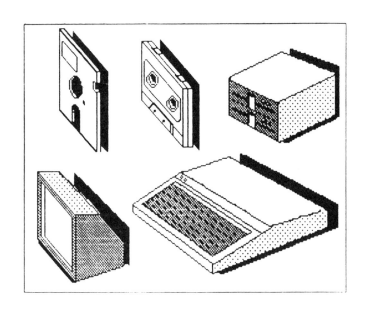

Fig. 3.2

product. Again skills in thinking about information, creating and using information, cooperative skills, planning skills, design skills and editing skills can all be strengthened by the use of such programs. As was seen with EDFAX and COMMUNITEL, the applications in various subjects (e.g. FLEET STREET EDITOR has maps in its Graphics Library which could be used in Geography) are limitless and school librarians and teachers can encourage pupils to use the technology in a new and educationally productive way.

Information

Part of the school librarian's role is to market the services offered by the school library and the use of the software packages cited in this chapter can improve the quality of output of the information produced for staff and pupils.

Word processing can help in producing subject-based bibliographies, abstracts of new books or articles of relevance to teachers, interim reports on the use of the library, worksheets used by the librarian and teachers in information skills programmes and general notices about library facilities.

Using teletext emulator packages, the school librarian has the facility to produce information in electronic and printed form. While this will not improve the quality of the *content* of the information, it can be used to attract attention to displays of information in a way in which printed notices or guides cannot. By using pupils to create graphics, school librarians can transfer actual displays of new material on to the screen, for example, by recreating book covers or pages from CAL software. These pages can be shown not only in the school library but also in the staffroom by setting up a microcomputer system in the staffroom and allowing staff to use either the interactive COMMUNITEL pages or by using new software packages. In this way, the school librarian is taking an active role in information dissemination and marketing the library 'products' in a new and effective way.

By allowing pupils access to the school library microcomputer and packages such as FLEET STREET EDITOR, the school librarian can transform the school library into an information centre where the information for pupils is created and designed by the pupils and used by pupils in the library. Also, by using print-outs from various packages, notices using text and graphics can be produced for noticeboards throughout the school.

This chapter has shown the uses of different software packages for administrative and curricular purposes. Many uses of the software are as yet, undiscovered, because although a software package is designed for one purpose, it can be adapted to meet a particular need

40

within a school which the software designers had not thought about. By giving pupils access to such software, the educational aim of allowing creative thought and action can be achieved by school librarians and teachers.

References
1. Costa, B. and Costa, M., *A micro handbook*, Libraries Unlimited, 1983, 61.
2. Megarry, J., 'An introduction to Wordwise Plus', *Computer Concepts*, 1984.
3. Stonier, T. and Conlin, T., *The three Cs*, Wiley, 1985, 75.
4. Papert, S., *Mindstorms*. Harvester Press, 1981, 31. In: Stonier and Conlin, *op. cit.*, 66.
5. Askey, J., 'Prestel education at Houghton Regis Upper School', *PRESTEL Education*, 1986.
6. Astill, M. *et al.*, 'Edfax teletext emulator', *Tecmedia*, 1984, 5.
7. Mercer, S. and Bitton, P., 'Fleet Street Editor', *Mirrorsoft*, 1986, Al. 5.

Chapter 4
Issue systems on the microcomputer
by Renee Deans

Case study 1: Falmer High School

Falmer School is a fairly large, split-site comprehensive school on the outskirts of Brighton catering for 11 – 18-year-olds. It is organized into upper and lower schools with a library in each building. In January 1985, it became obvious that with the loss of the librarian in the South Library, it was necessary to investigate the automation of the loans system, this being the only way in which any form of lending service could be maintained in the lower school.

Until this point, the issue system was a modified Browne charging system based on a weekly rather than a daily record. This had the advantage of being simple to operate and relatively cheap. It was, however, very labour intensive and therefore expensive in term of staff hours in operating the system and particularly in issuing overdue notices.

Various organizations were contacted to find out if they had any details of library issue systems using CBM or BBC microcomputers, both of which were already available in the school. Unfortunately, they did not have information on any program which would deal with a small issue of some 500 items. The school could not afford the time or expense of putting bar-codes on all stock in both libraries. Also, if such a system were put into operation, a member of staff would be needed to operate the light-pen in the South Library and every pupil and teacher would need an individual borrower card. As most school librarians have experience of pupils losing library tickets, it was estimated that individual cards would need replacing regularly. Also, to use a light-pen system would require the production of a database of the total library stock and of all individual users. The technology required to cope with this would be far beyond the capabilities of the microcomputers present in the school and the cost of hardware and software needed to run such a system would be prohibitive.

The software eventually found to meet the school's needs and limited financial and staffing resources, was LIBRAFILE, an issue system designed to run on a 48K BBC-B microcomputer. The software was inexpensive and could run on a single or dual disk drive system. It was decided that the school should purchase the software

42

and run a pilot scheme to discover whether or not it was a viable proposition.

At this stage, a method of obtaining loans data from pupils had to be discovered. The system chosen was a form which asked for the name of the pupil, their form, and the author and title of the book borrowed. To return a book, a form giving the name and form number of the borrower was required. This form would then be placed inside the book and the book 'posted' into a locked container. The loan slips would then be used to enter the data into the microcomputer and they were filed in alphabetical order by title. When the book was returned, the loan slip would be removed from the alphabetical system and used to delete the loan from the microcomputer. The slips are shown in Figures 4.1 and 4.2.

Figure 4.1: Loan slip form

FALMER SCHOOL LIBRARY

BORROWERS NAME   FORM

TITLE

AUTHOR   DATE BORROWED

Figure 4.2: Return slip form

FALMER SCHOOL LIBRARY

BOOKS RETURNED TO THE LIBRARY

NAME OF BORROWER:

FORM

Running the system

This program is available on disk and on a ROM chip. The advantage of using the disk version is that it can be run on different BBC microcomputers whereas the chip, being inside one microcomputer, is less flexible. The LIBRAFILE disk contains the programs needed to run the system and also a datafile primed to receive the information generated by loans. The datafile is able to deal with up to four hundred records at any one time and it is at this stage that the school librarian has to decide on the number of data disks which will be needed. The crucial figure in this decision is the maximum number of loans at any one time.

When LIBRAFILE is purchased, the librarian has to make a copy of the master disk for day to day use. It is important that this is done immediately, as the master disk cannot be copied once it has been used. Thus it is very important to read the instructions carefully when using programs of this nature. Once the master disk has been copied, the program can be run. The program itself is very simple to use and is menu-driven. The program has eight options which are displayed once the program is loaded and the librarian answers questions on the screen. These questions relate to whether the school is using a single or dual disk drive and what type of printer is being used. In terms of printer use, the librarian has to state whether s/he is using

1) Parallel (Centronics output)
   or
2) Serial (RS423 output)

Most printers will be parallel and this can be easily checked by looking at the microcomputer. If the printer interface is connected to the printer slot on the underside of the BBC microcomputer, then it is parallel. The RS423 socket is on the back of the microcomputer.

The user then has to input the date and it is against this date that all transactions will be checked. The list of options are shown in Figure 4.3

Figure 4.3: Input Options

1. Check all data
2. List data
3. Enter a record
4. Obtain status report
5. Search the records
6. Print reminders
7. Change the data disks
8. Leave the program

Option 1 allows the librarian to check all the data stored on the disk i.e. how many items are on loan and allows a scan through items which might be overdue.

Option 2 allows the user to have a printed list of all the books or items on loan to a particular year, class, individual or by a particular author. Figure 4.4 shows a print-out for a search by pupil name and by author. This could be useful in checking the range of fiction books borrowed by pupils or a subject teacher may wish to examine the types of material borrowed for a particular project by a class.

Figure 4.4: Print-out for search by pupil name and author

Falmer School Library
List produced on 22 October 1986
Books on loan to Stephen Moulson
Title   :   Superbikes
Author   :   Carrick P
Due back :   06 October 1986

Option 3 is used for entering records and is used when pupils borrow materials from the school library. The user answers the prompts on the screen and the program works out the date for return (21 days after the date of loan). The entry is then displayed on screen for correction and if it is correct, the librarian chooses option 3 and the data is written on to the disk. A prompt then appears for the next entry. If there are no more loans to be entered, the user presses the RETURN key and goes back to the options list. Figure 4.5 shows the screen display for entering records.

Figure 4.5: Screen display for entering records

First name   Surname

Form   Author's name

Book title

Type in data in the order given
pressing RETURN after each item
PRESS 'ESCAPE' TO RETURN TO MENU

Option 4 gives a status report and is useful in collecting statistics on the use of the library over a period of two years. The school librarian is provided with a monthly total of items borrowed over the previous two years and a running total of items on loan to each year group. This allows the librarian to gauge use of the library in total and the use made by particular classes. It will also reveal, by default, which classes are *not* using the school library on a regular basis and the school librarian may wish to find out the reasons for this lack of use. Figures 4.6 and 4.7 illustrate the types of information provided.

Figure 4.6: Status Report

Status report for 10 September 1986.
There are 230 books on loan.
Of these 10% are overdue.

Books on loan to year groups

Year	Books on loan	Books overdue	%
1	51	11	20
2	48	0	0
3	36	0	0
4	62	0	0
5	33	12	28

SPACE BAR FOR NEXT PAGE

Figure 4.7: Use of library

	1986	1985
January	294	287
February	356	342
March	312	316
April	167	157
May	321	298
June	290	294
July	210	199
August	36	23
September	269	298
October	0	319
November	0	340
December	0	343

Total number of books borrowed per month during 1985 and 1986.

SPACE BAR TO CONTINUE

Option 5 allows the user to search the records. This can be used to discharge loans when books or items are returned. A search is made by pupil's name or by the title of an item. When the details are displayed on screen, the data can be deleted from the file by choosing 2 on the screen or if the book is to be renewed, the date can be changed by choosing 1. The option is useful if a user, either teacher or pupil wishes to know whether a particular title is on loan (it could be misshelved) or who has a particular title. The school librarian and teachers will have to decide on a policy relating to this information – should other pupils know which particular pupil has a particular book? Revealing such information could produce problems for the pupils with a book which is in demand. Figure 4.8 outlines the steps in this option.

Figure 4.8: Search Program

        Do you want to search for a pupil?
(The user presses Y or N)
If N
        Do you want to search for a book title?
(The user presses Y or N. If N, the user is taken back to the menu.)

Option 6 allows the librarian to have overdue reminders printed out by the microcomputer and in terms of time saved, this is one of the attractions of a computerized loans system. The microcomputer will print out reminders for all items which are overdue on a particular date and the reminders can be sent to pupils via the form or year tutor. Figure 4.9 shows a print-out of a reminder.

Figure 4.9: Reminder print-out

Falmer School Library

Pupil's name: Anthony White   Form: 412

The book 'The Vietnam War' on loan to you from the library is now overdue. Please return it as soon as possible.

Option 7 allows the user to change data disks but the librarian must ensure that this option is chosen *before* the old data disk is removed from the disk drive.

Option 8 is used to leave the program and must be selected to ensure that all the data is safely stored. The user must not switch off the computer before this option is chosen as this could affect further use of the files on disk.

Benefits

A computerized loans system such as LIBRAFILE is beneficial to the school librarian, particularly in the time saved in issuing reminder notices. It also helps with the image of the school library in that the school librarian is seen to be using new technology to improve the efficiency of the school library. Pupils also benefit by experiencing another use of technology which may be outside their own experience.

LIBRAFILE produces instant information on the status of books and borrowers which is very difficult with a manual system. The statistics on use of the library over a period can prove useful in presenting reports to the school hierarchy and arguing for increases in resources.

The software also has many limitations as seen above. It is *not* comparable to mainframe systems such as Plessey, Telepen or GEAC because of the hardware used. It is also inflexible in that the period of loan cannot be altered and certain information cannot be printed out. Pupils still have to fill in forms for issue and discharge of material but the problems with library tickets are avoided.

Using a microcomputer for a loans system has proved a valuable introduction to new technology for this school librarian, in that she has gained new skills which can be used to exploit the resources of the school library. Having used the microcomputer for this purpose the school librarian is now planning to use word processing programs and to link an information retrieval program to the school's information skills course, thus expanding the use of the microcomputer into *educational* as well as administrative areas.

Case study 2: Sacred Heart Comprehensive School
The school is an all-girls, comprehensive school in Newcastle Upon Tyne and has two libraries on the upper and lower sites of the school. The school librarian, Mr Les Rae, was approached by MEP in December 1985 and asked to pilot the EDLIB software which had been developed locally. The software is a microcomputer-based library system designed for schools and colleges and can operate the issue, return and cataloguing of up to 65,000 books for 2,500 users. In terms of issue, EDLIB uses bar-code labels and a bar-code reader. When a pupil borrows or returns a book, the bar-code reader is drawn across the bar-code on the book or item and across the pupil's bar-coded library ticket. This is similar to systems used in many public and academic libraries and eschews the need for each pupil to have separate library tickets.

The EDLIB system works as a cataloguing system as well as an issue system and the issue system works from a Titles File which is created at the cataloguing stage. In the school, the fiction section of the lower school was catalogued first. Each book was accessioned and the catalogue data entered into the microcomputer. The library has two assistants, one on each site but with the help of the sixth-form pupils, 1500 books were processed in two weeks. At the same time, the lower school User File, containing details of all pupils likely to borrow items from this library, was created. The pupils' details were entered on to disk, each pupil was assigned a unique number and bar-codes were produced. Figure 4.10 shows a bar-code for a book and for a pupil.

The issue system will issue and discharge books and items in the normal way but can also be used to search for information and to produce overdues. The system can be searched by author, title or pupils's name, as seen with LIBRAFILE above and overdues can be produced for a pupil, a class or for the whole school.

One of the advantages of EDLIB is that it acts as a computerized catalogue as well as an issue system. The catalogue system creates files in which each book or audiovisual item is allocated a record, which contains accession number, title, author, Dewey number, price, subject and one spare field, which can be used as another subject field. In Sacred Heart School, the non-fiction section of the lower school was catalogued first and subject codes were assigned to each item. The librarian involved the pupils in this task as much as possible, as they were the intended users of the system. A thesaurus was created by the pupils to use with the subject keys as an aid to searching the catalogue. Each book or item has two subject keys. The first subject key reflects the curricular context e.g. physics or geography and the second subject key is more general. Each subject key is restricted to three letters and a pupil searching for information on WATER might search under PHY and WAT for materials on WATER in relation to PHYSICS or under WAT to search for anything on WATER. Pupils will be encouraged to use printed lists of keywords when the system is fully operational. One difficuly here is to create keys for subjects which begin with the same first three letters e.g. FARMING and FAROES but the school librarian sees this as a useful information problem for pupils to tackle.

EDLIB is a more sophisticated package than LIBRAFILE and is also more expensive. EDLIB also requires the use of dual track, double-sided disk drives and a BBC-B microcomputer. Both systems present school librarians with the possibilities of using the microcomputer to provide more sophisticated and streamlined services to their users.

Fig. 4.10

49

Chapter 5
Database creation
by Dorothy A Williams

Introduction

It might be said that 'database creation' means different things to different people. To a school librarian, the term might conjour up the image of compiling a computerized catalogue with details of resources held in the school library. For some teachers, 'database creation' might well bring to mind a class using microcomputers as an efficient means of collating, storing and retrieving information about the local environment, about 19th century village life or about the class itself. For secondary school pupils, database creation may as yet mean very little outside the computer studies department but, on encountering some examples of databases in S1/S2, they may remember similar exercises with football teams or animals in primary school.

The type of information and the purpose of the exercise of database creation may mean different things but underlying these examples, there is a general concept central to *all* – that of using a microcomputer to store information in a way which provides rapid, flexible and specific access and which meets the needs of potential users.

Also, the *processes* and skills involved in the creation of a database, be it computerized or 'manual', are similar for all the above examples. In exploring these processes, the school librarian, teachers and pupils can learn from one another and, more importantly, they can *learn together*.

In looking at the process of database creation, the value of databases in the school library will be seen to extend beyond immediate access to specific information. The processes outlined and the examples used are based on work done in the MISLIP project in Scottish secondary schools but similar work has been done throughout the UK.

Why create databases in the school library?

The major role of the school librarian or resources manager is to provide access to the kind of information users require and, especially in schools, to help users develop the skills which will enable them to identify the purpose of, find and use that information.

This is becoming increasingly important with the move towards more independent learning within the school curriculum. Pupils' active involvement in the learning process is important in enhancing their knowledge and understanding in many subject areas.

The rapid expansion in the levels of information available in society also makes it increasingly important that pupils begin to develop an awareness of the wealth of information available and the skills and confidence which will allow them to make use of the information *after* they leave school.

With this in mind, those concerned with information management in schools need to be aware of any new technologies which can assist in the development of learning skills which are relevant across and beyond the curriculum. The microcomputer as an *information retrieval tool* is already seen by many teachers and librarians as one means of encouraging and motivating pupils to become more involved in information handling assignments while also helping them develop information retrieval skills.

The microcomputer has certain advantages over manual forms of information retrieval. These may be summed up as speed, accuracy and flexibility in retrieving information. The user has greater freedom to structure searches to suit individual needs. By keying in one or a number of search terms e.g. subject keywords, author or format, the user can broaden or narrow a search without any predesigned classification structure. This places emphasis on *thinking* about *purpose* and structuring searches to meet information needs, an emphasis which can be beneficial in selecting and rejecting information after using the microcomputer i.e. in reading, note making, and organizing information.

The creation of a database in the school library can therefore be seen as something *more* than the provision of a catalogue of resources. Through the use of curriculum-related databases holding factual or bibliographic information, the microcomputer can bring the library closer to the curriculum in terms of content and skills. At the same time, pupils are also exposed to one practical application of the microcomputer which will be relevant outside school.

What is a database?

Before looking at the creation of databases, it is important to consider what is meant by a database or what a database could look like in a school library.

A database is simply a collection of information, factual or bibliographic, numerical or alphabetic, and textual or graphic. In the context of the microcomputer, a database is a collection of information held in one or more *files* on disk. Each file has a unique name by which it is accessed.

Within a file, information is organized in a number of records, rather like the cards in a card index. Each of these records is divided up into a number of fields, each holding one item of information such as name or address, or author or title.

Limits on space devoted to each record and the number of fields in each record will vary depending on the hardware and software used. Some databases may have all the information in one record held in one large field e.g. Prestel, COMMUNITEL or MICROVIEWDATA databases, while database management programs may have a number of fields all of which can be accessed individually e.g. KWIRS, SIR, QUEST or MASTERFILE. This gives the basis for a very specific and flexible information retrieval system which, within the constraints of the hardware and software available, can be structured and designed to suit the kind of information in the database and the needs of users.

The examples below fall into the latter category and were created by school librarians and teachers in the MISLIP project.

How is a database created?

The process of creating a database can be divided into two basic stages – *design* and *development*. Throughout the process and particularly in the design stage, the focus is on the user group – those who will potentially be accessing the information contained in the database and their likely purpose in using it. This is no different from the design of any other information retrieval system. Database creation is the process of matching the capacity, features and potential of the hardware and software to the needs of those who will be using the system and the information it contains.

Design

Even with the simplest database management program for microcomputers used in schools, there is a great deal of flexibility for the design of databases to suit particular needs. These may be large- or small-scale databases designed with very specific educational aims, to cater for a particular topic or part of a course, or for more general use in the school library. The kind of hardware generally available at present is ideally suited to small-scale database creation i.e. databases with 200-800 records. The school librarian or teacher is not therefore dealing with a traditional cataloguing and indexing task whereby one system is adhered to within the information retrieval system, as in a card catalogue. Each database will cover a specific topic and is likely to have its own set of potential uses. To achieve maximum benefit in terms of information skills and the use of information, each database should be seen as a separate entity as far as the *design* of the records and indexing is concerned, although an overall pattern for database use within the school is beneficial.

The important decisions to be reached at the design stage may be seen in terms of five basic questions:

a) What is the general theme or topic?
b) Who is likely to use the information?
c) What kinds of question will they ask?
d) What kind of information will they need?
e) What should the information look like?

These questions are not in themselves new and may be familiar to anyone who has had to design a catalogue, prepare a report, give a talk or write an essay. The unfamiliar part of the process lies in relating these questions to a computerized end product.

a) What is the general theme or topic?

The choice of topic or subject area can be influenced by many factors. It is important, for example, to have cooperation between the school librarian and the teacher during the planning stages – the aims and content of the curriculum and the knowledge and ability of pupils is important at *all* stages of development – and choice of topic may therefore be partly determined by a particular teacher.

The topic or theme influences the size and scope of the database. A database on WATER, for example, might have endless scope for variation and extension into several curricular areas while a database on the TUDOR PERIOD may have more restricted use.

The first database produced in a school library may be deliberately small in size, and provide an opportunity to examine all angles of *creation* and use before tackling a much larger subject.

b) Who is likely to use the information?

Knowledge of the user group is of particular importance and influences the content, layout and indexing of a database. Factors such as age, reading ability, knowledge of indexes, knowledge of audiovisual equipment, and previous experience in finding and using resources and information may all have to be taken into account if the database is to act as a link between purpose and information.

If, for example, the pupils who are likely to use a database have reading problems, it is important to produce a 'readable' record with each element of information clearly spaced out. If users have little experience of using videocassette recorders or tape-slide equipment, a decision may have to be made on whether to ignore sources such as videocassettes or tape-slide sets which may be relevant to the database or to include such materials but ensure that help and guidance are available when the equipment is needed.

c) What kind of questions will they ask?

Knowledge of the curriculum is important in the *indexing* of a database. The choice of access points or retrieval fields and the specific terminology used to 'label' each record depends on the content, aims and objectives of the curriculum.

The words, ideas or questions in a pupil's mind – the words used to express a need for information – are derived from classroom discussion, introductory materials, worksheets and the language used by the teacher. These are important starting points in the development of an indexing language.

In most cases, the need for information is expressed in *subject* rather than bibliographic details (one exception often being fiction) and the development of a curriculum-based indexing language is one of the most important aspects of the design of a database. The aims and objectives of the curriculum and the particular assignment – the specific areas the pupils are expected to explore, the scope for individual research and the expected outcome of the task – will largely determine the depth of keyword indexing as well as coverage of the database.

Selection of keywords is often easier for a more structured assignment or where more 'concrete' concepts are being dealt with. A database for a short exercise on the scientific properties of WATER may, for example, be easier to index initially than one for a project on the lives and achievements of famous people, where there may be greater scope for individual interpretation. On the other hand, the latter assignment may demand more from a pupil in terms of information retrieval and may be a more fruitful area for database creation.

Pupils themselves can be valuable sources of keywords, not only in terms of written work produced in class but also in the language used in discussion and in asking questions in the classroom or in the school library. Whether initially or after piloting a database, pupils can often suggest keywords which have been missed by the librarian or teacher at the planning stage.

It is helpful for the indexer to have an understanding not only of important concepts but also the *relationships* between concepts within the structure of a topic. A keyword map (see Chapter 6) or thesaurus can be an advantage not only in the initial construction of a database but also, on a long term basis, in updating the database.

In bibliographic databases, it is important to consider whether pupils will want or need to search for a particular author, a particular location or a particular format such as 'book' or 'video'. While in most cases this will be unnecessary for pupils, it may initially be an advantage for the school librarian or teacher for producing lists from the database. For example, a teacher may wish to have a list of books used in a particular project.

d) *What kind of information will they need?*
This question again relates to the needs and abilities of users as well as the aims and objectives of the curriculum. A database may hold *factual* information e.g. facts about Eskimo life or important Eskimo words and their meaning or it may hold *bibliographic* information (fiction or non-fiction) e.g. references to books, slide-sets, films, or periodical articles on Eskimo life and their environment. The kind of information relevant to users depends on the nature of their assignment or course, whether there is time and opportunity to use resources or whether the database is seen as the information source.

Factual databases can be a useful way of introducing keyword searching. Pupils can use the immediate feedback of information to evaluate the success of their search strategy and broaden or narrow their search as appropriate. While working with factual databases can have a bearing on pupils' skill in using bibliographic databases, it may also serve to reinforce previous database use in the primary school classroom.

In bibliographic databases, the school librarian and teacher must consider whether it is necessary or desirable to include features such as publication details, page references and notes. The need to encourage pupils to evaluate and select resources and information and to use indexes must be balanced against the number of selection stages with which the pupils can cope. The use of any database should be seen within the overall pattern of information skills development within the school.

e) *What should the information look like?*
The layout of each record, whether single field as in Prestel or multiple field as in KWIRS or SIR, whether factual or bibliographic, will influence the ease with which pupils can *use* the information. Depending on the software available, there may be options to use colour, contrast, and upper and lower case letters to highlight headings or field names. Even where such scope is limited, the use of *space* and punctuation can be important in producing a readable and understandable record.

Any decisions must balance the needs and abilities of users with the type and quality of information to held in the database.

Development

While collaboration between the teacher and the school librarian is essential in the design of the database, the selection and indexing of information and resources, and the construction and maintenance of a database are usually seen as the tasks of the school librarian. In schools where there is no full-time librarian, it could still be done by teachers.

If adequate time has been spent at the design stage, the construction of files holds few major problems. The process of selecting relevant resources and/or information and keywording or 'classifying' the information will not be new to school librarians. The 'new' aspect lies in entering the information at the microcomputer keyboard, having specified the number of fields, field names and position of fields in each record according to the design decisions reached earlier. If the software documentation is readable and understandable, this should be largely a matter of following instructions.

The most important ingredient in the construction stage is *time* but, although this is sometimes a source of worry at the beginning, in practice it is often found that this stage is *less* time-consuming than the planning stages. Approaches to selection, organization and database construction vary according to the day to day timetable of a school library and it is important in selecting a topic to consider the time-scale of the project. Where one librarian may choose to spend several complete days in the school vacation creating a database, other librarians or teachers may choose to spend a few hours every week over one or two terms.

Often in the initial stages of database development new keywords can be suggested by the materials being indexed or particular design features may need to be altered once the information can be viewed on screen or in a print-out. It is often helpful to create several small files (5-10 entries maximum) with varying layouts and indexing as an aid to discussion at the design stage. This serves to clarify issues for both the school librarian and the teacher and can be a valuable time-saving device in the long term.

Case studies

Many of the major points raised in the design and development of databases hinge on the need to consider curriculum, users and information in the planning stages.

The case studies below illustrate how the aims and objectives of the curriculum and the needs and abilities of users have influenced the design of three databases produced in schools who are participating in the MISLIP project.

A. Medieval village – an S1 history project in Cumnock Academy
The database was created for a structured approach to a project or short guided exercises on themes connected with life in a medieval village. Each of the records in this short (54 records) file contains a question or task to be carried out using the reference(s) given.

Main access is by keyword on three levels designed to cater for varying approaches depending on time available, the abilities of pupils and the emphasis placed on the theme in each class.

Pupils can be guided to an *item* (see Figure 5.1) such as SHIPS which will retrieve one record with a task relating to that specific theme and to one or two sources of information.

A lengthier, yet structured project can be built up around a *category* keyword (the first keyword field) such as TRANSPORT, leading the pupil to four or five records containing tasks and references on different aspects or 'items' of TRANSPORT.

The second keyword field contains additional 'clue' keywords which provide more information about the specific references as well as expanding the scope of the inquiry and providing for a more flexible approach to a project.

In designing the database, the *category* and *item* keywords were closely defined by the activities of the unit prepared by the teacher and the school librarian. The 'clue' keywords were added by the librarian after considering the coverage of the history unit up to this point. This field therefore represents keywords likely to be meaningful to pupils, based on their background work on the topic, and may be particularly important where a more flexible approach to project work is taken.

While titles and locations have been placed in retrieval fields, this has been done to emphasize these elements and to stress the ideas of *sources* of information, seen as an important concept in history teaching. These features are of secondary importance in searching the database in this assignment.

This school is now using databases in the history (S1-S6), science, English and music curricula, while further databases are being planned for English and art.

Each file has been designed by the librarian and teachers to cater for the specific needs and aims of the curriculum and pupils. This has resulted in a range of different record designs, headings and depth of indexing as well as the use of factual and bibliographic information as appropriate. The use of the same hardware and software (BBC-B and

47.
How is the stage strange? Do Exs 3&4 in Everyday Life p25. Make a poster
advertising a play.

```
ITEM.............PLAYS
KEYWORDS.........PASTIMES
                 STAGE
SOURCE...........Everyday Life
                 in Middle Ages
                 p47
                 Living in
                 the Past
                 p24-25
LOCATION.........940.1
```

4.
Describe how ploughing improved at this time. Why could horses do more work
on the land?

```
ITEM.............PLOUGHING
KEYWORDS ........WORK
                 HORSES
SOURCE...........Medieval
                 Times
                 p22-23

LOCATION.........940.1
```

3.
Describe the role of the priest. What would you like and dislike about his
life?

```
ITEM.............PRIEST
KEYWORDS.........RELIGION
                 TITHE
SOURCE...........Living in
                 Medieval Village
                 p22-23
                 Living in
                 the Past
                 p26-27
LOCATION.........940.1
```

Fig. 5.1

KWIRS) each time, means that emphasis will be placed on the
information aspect rather than the *technological* aspects of the
information retrieval system.

Figure 5.1 shows a print-out of records from a file in the medieval
village database.

B. S2 Humanities project (on human rights movements) in Bankhead Academy, Aberdeen
This project allows pupils great freedom to structure their own
research into some aspect of the life of Gandhi, Mother Teresa of
Calcutta or Martin Luther King Junior. The database for the project

58

therefore has a very wide coverage, with the background work in class suggesting links with religion, slavery and the history and geography of India and the United States. The only restriction in materials to be included was the level of difficulty and some of the more advanced texts were withdrawn from the database after the first pilot use. The database of approximately 180 references includes audiovisual and print materials held in the school library.

The retrieval emphasis is on *keywords* (see Figure 5.2) and *author* with in-depth indexing to allow for specific and flexible searching. The aim is to help pupils develop information retrieval skills by allowing them scope to experiment and develop search strategies according to their own interests and purposes within the project.

With the wide coverage and freedom given to pupils to develop their own individual lines of inquiry, the identification of a large and detailed collection of keywords was one of the major tasks at the design stage. The indexing language was added to during the construction of the database as more aspects were suggested by the materials. After piloting the database, three keywords were added to the file, representing aspects of the life of the three main characters which had been particularly important to several pupils but had not been catered for initially. The provision of a checklist of keywords has been more important in the use of this database than might be the case in a more structured and guided assignment.

The record design indicates that, as in other databases in this

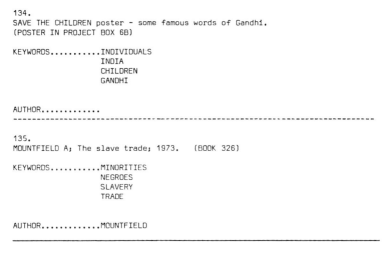

```
134.
SAVE THE CHILDREN poster - some famous words of Gandhi.
(POSTER IN PROJECT BOX 6B)

KEYWORDS...........INDIVIDUALS
                   INDIA
                   CHILDREN
                   GANDHI


AUTHOR............
---------------------------------------------------------------------------
135.
MOUNTFIELD A; The slave trade; 1973.   (BOOK 326)

KEYWORDS...........MINORITIES
                   NEGROES
                   SLAVERY
                   TRADE


AUTHOR............MOUNTFIELD
```

Fig. 5.2

school, *date* is the only publication detail felt to be appropriate at the S1/S2 stage.

Page references have been included in this file as, although pupils have covered indexes in their information skills course, this was one of the first occasions when they were asked to take much of the responsibility for their own project. Teachers felt that it was more appropriate to help pupils move as quickly as possible from purposes to information, with emphasis on reading and note making skills at that stage.

Pupils using this database have already explored the use of keywords and questions to define information needs, to read for information and to summarize and organize information. This is one of several fiction and non-fiction databases available in the school library. Others include an S2 science database on STREAMLINING and an S2 modern studies database on the KALAHARI. Pupils are also involved in creating small factual and/or fiction databases with the same information retrieval program (KWIRS) as is used in the resources databases. Over a period of time, therefore, pupils are exposed to different aspects of the microcomputer as an information retrieval tool and are developing an awareness of the crucial link between purpose and information.

Figure 5.2 shows examples from the database and illustrates the difference in layout from that in Figure 5.1, which emphasizes the flexibility open to school librarians and teachers in using information retrieval programs on microcomputers.

C. Cave man – an S1 learning support project in Dunbar Grammar School

In this project, pupils were asked to investigate aspects of stone age man and write up their findings in booklet form. The database was created to meet the needs of learning support pupils with very low reading ages (7-9 years). It was important not only to provide clearly *readable* records in the file (101 entries) but also to provide clear links between the purposes defined by pupils and the information in the books. With this in mind there was a heavy emphasis on *questions* used in class to guide reading and projects, and on important keywords (see Figure 5.3).

The questions and keywords were provided by the teacher *and* pupils in the early stages of this unit. Four different layouts were experimented with until the final version of the file (Figure 5.3) was arrived at. Each version shows variation on the idea of providing keywords and questions in indexing terms. The final version relies on keyword access, with pupils selecting keywords from questions they

```
1.
McCORD.A. EARLY MAN.   573.3 S.L.S.    Beliefs page 24 - tools pages 22-23 -
weapons pages 22-23 - fishing page 23.

TOPICS...........BELIEFS
                 TOOLS
                 WEAPONS
                 FISHING
_____

1.
HINDE.C.  THE FIRST MEN ON EARTH.          573.3 S.L.S. PAGE23.

QUESTION.........WHAT
                 DID
                 THEY
                 KILL
                 WITH?

KEYWORD..........HUNTING
_____

1.
How did they make ornaments?        What did they make ornaments from?
LOWTHER.K.  EARLY MAN.   573.3 S.L.S.    PART 10

KEYWORDS.........ORNAMENTS
_____

13.
HOMES
How did they make their homes       Where did they live?
                                    MILLARD.A.  EARLY MAN. PAGE 48.

KEYWORD..........HOMES
SHELF NUMBER.....573.3.  S.L.S.
```

Fig. 5.3

have posed as a group and being referred to specific questions in the main body of each record.

Bibliographic details have been kept to a minimum, with enough for pupils to recognize a book by author, title and classification number from the small selection provided on loan by the local school library service. Page references were necessary for this so that pupils could quickly move from purpose to information. Emphasis was placed on encouraging *reading* at this stage and selection of resources and the use of indexes was minimized.

The database has been used by one group of learning support pupils who have used the print-outs not only to find the books they want but also to organize their projects, using the questions as section headings.

Figure 5.3 demonstrates the ability of the school librarian and teacher to discuss different layouts of information to meet the special needs of a specific group of pupils.

In all the above case studies, the importance of liaison between the school librarian and teacher is clear. An understanding of the curriculum and the needs of different groups of pupils is essential to the success of any curriculum-related database, while an awareness of the skills required to find and use information is an important factor for any teacher setting an assignment which involves pupils in information handling.

The two-way exchange of specialized knowledge can bring benefits to the school librarian, teachers and pupils. Librarians see advantages in terms of increased use of resources, increased interest and involvement of pupils and teachers in the library, a chance to identify accurately information needs and an enhancement of pupils' abilities to locate and use pertinent information sources. Teachers can benefit from the opportunity afforded to develop pupils' information skills within the context of the curriculum and to encourage pupils to become actively involved in the learning process. A major factor here is that pupils *enjoy* finding information.

In terms of pupils development, a database should be seen as an integral part of an assignment and part of a *long term, cross-curricular development* of information skills. The process of database creation can itself be valuable experience for pupils, introducing them to the information retrieval system, while encouraging the use of many information skills. Through the creation and use of databases in a number of different contexts over a period of time, pupils develop an awareness of the microcomputer as an information handling tool rather than a games machine or programming instrument, while, at the same time, developing valuable learning skills.

It is important, therefore, in creating a database in the school library or classroom, to begin with a clear statement of aims and objectives relating to the design of the database and the needs and abilities of users. This process should bring together school librarian and teacher, library and curriculum and the database in the context of information use in school and outside.

Chapter 6
Microcomputers and information skills
by Sandra G Davison

'The heart and soul of a resource collection is not material at all: it lies in the structure of thought it exhibits, in the creative association it provokes and in the opportunities it provides for training the young learner in how to learn and think.'[1]

Introduction
In recent years there have been changes in educational emphasis in schools. Resource-based learning has placed greater importance on learning how to learn and the handling of information. The introduction of the microcomputer, and in particular the BBC range, is also bringing about fundamental change and development within the curriculum.

Schools are '. . . an environment in which information is not only the key raw material and manipulative tool: it is also the key product'[2] and in the educational environment of the 1980s where TVEI, CPVE, GCSE, 16+ and Standard Grade (see Glossary) are providing opportunities for pupils to become increasingly sophisticated users of information sources and systems, the ability to handle information is becoming an important skill.

One of the four main aims of MEP states that, '. . . use should be made of the microcomputer to develop the individual's capacity for independent learning and information retrieval'[3] and computerized information retrieval in school libraries can provide such a learning situation through the successful integration of curricular needs and information sources.

Though there are many disadvantages as well as advantages in the use of microcomputers for information retrieval, the major advantage is that computerized information retrieval can provide a strong link between the school library and the curriculum by increasing pupils' exposure to new technologies as both a learning and retrieval tool, regardless of subject area, and increase the use of resources in the school.

Background
At Milne's High School, the use of the microcomputer for information retrieval and for providing opportunities for pupils to

develop keyword skills, is an important part of the school library policy. From first year, pupils are encouraged to use the microcomputer to locate fiction books and this is reinforced in the Modern Studies syllabus, later English work, and by the Art department. Experimental work on pupil-created data files was also carried out in the 1983-4 session in a small research project.[4]

Work in the Modern Studies department began with an experimental datafile based on 'Parliament' in 1983-4 and is gradually extending to cover the proposed Standard Grade framework. Work with second-year pupils on 'Housing' and 'Alternative ideologies' will see the combination of both databases (using EDFAX) and datafiles, in those parts of the curriculum where pupils are expected to carry out inquiry work.

Aims and objectives

1. To produce datafiles relevant to the Modern Studies syllabus by creating curriculum-based access to all useful information within the school.

2. To provide an opportunity for pupils to use and extend inquiry and communication skills developed in class work.

3. To examine problems in developing curriculum-based databases and datafiles.

4. To integrate concept/keyword skills to both the Modern Studies syllabus and information skills material.

5. To create databases that contain local statistics and are tailored to the needs of particular units of work within the curriculum.

Learning outcomes

1. Pupils learn to view the microcomputer as an important tool in the successful retrieval of both references and specific information.

2. Pupils develop the ability to negotiate a search strategy for computerized information retrieval both as individuals and as members of a group.

3. Pupils are capable of articulating a need for information and expressing that need in terms of curriculum-based concepts and keywords.

4. Pupils see the microcomputer as
a) a source of information (as in databases)
b) sources of reference (as in datafiles)
c) a learning and communicating medium

Datafiles – syllabus areas and compulsory topics

Work initially concentrated on the production of data files for the compulsory topics within the Modern Studies syllabus. This was a deliberate choice, enhancing the transferability of the concepts/keyword work to other schools, should the opportunity arise to do so. The Modern Studies information system has now expanded to cover 16 syllabus topics, which are set out in Figure 6.1, and further datafiles are currently being planned.

Figure 6.1: Datafiles

Syllabus area	Datafile and number	
1. Politics in the UK	Elections	1/1
	Government	1/2
	Parliament	1/3
	Political parties	1/4
2. Social response to change	Employment patterns	2/1
	The Welfare State	2/2
3. International relations	Arms race	3/1
	E/W Relations	3/2
	Peace movements	3/3
	World Aid/Trade	3/4
4. Alternative ideologies	China	4/2
	Eastern Europe	4/3
	Eastern Europe – Human Rights	4/4
	USA	4/7
	USSR	4/8
	Western Europe	4/9

Database

The database being developed using the EDFAX teletext emulator program is based on work done by an informal group consisting of several schools and a college of education lecturer.[5] The group – the 'Housing Unit group' will be defining aims and objectives and Figure 6.2 provides a possible structure and content of the database.

Figure 6.2: Possible structure and content of a database

Future housing needs
Housing stocks in 1983
Local authority housing needs: 1983–8
Local authority sales
Rent and rates in 1983–4
Services and amenities
Sites proposed and started
Specialist housing

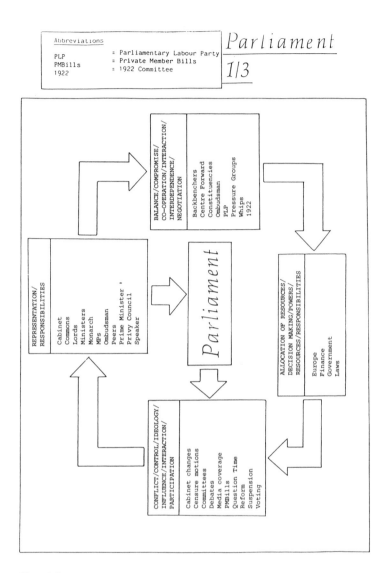

BALANCE/COMPROMISE/
CO-OPERATION/INTERACTION/
INTERDEPENDENCE/
NEGOTIATION

Backbenchers
Centre Forward
Constituencies
Ombudsman
PLP
Pressure Groups
Whips
1922

REPRESENTATION/
RESPONSIBILITIES

Cabinet
Commons
Lords
Ministers
Monarch
MPs
Ombudsman
Peers
Prime Minister
Privy Council
Speaker

Parliament

ALLOCATION OF RESOURCES/
DECISION MAKING/POWERS/
RESOURCES/RESPONSIBILITIES

Europe
Finance
Government
Laws

CONFLICT/CONTROL/IDEOLOGY/
INFLUENCE/INTERACTION/
PARTICIPATION

Cabinet changes
Censure motions
Committees
Debates
Media coverage
PMBills
Question Time
Reform
Suspension
Voting

Fig. 6.3

Concepts/keywords and inquiry/communicating skills
The outline syllabus for Standard Grade Modern Studies states that
'the most appropriate knowledge to be taught (will be the)
understanding of a group of interrelated concepts'[6] and in creating
the datafiles for Modern Studies, this statement has formed the basis

of keyword access and the learning of information skills for retrieving information using the microcomputer system.

Keywords are assigned to resources that match both pupil and teacher criteria, the inquiry/communicating skills required of pupils and the resources being indexed. They are then arranged in a concept/keyword map that combines the syllabus concepts and the relevant subject content of indexed resources. Each datafile has a corresponding concept/keyword map. The concepts used are too numerous to be shown in this chapter, but the example of a concept/keyword map in Figure 6.3 shows how concepts and keywords are combined into identifiable groups; and how concepts and keywords are interrelated. The impact of each group upon the others is shown by the spatial arrangement of groups.

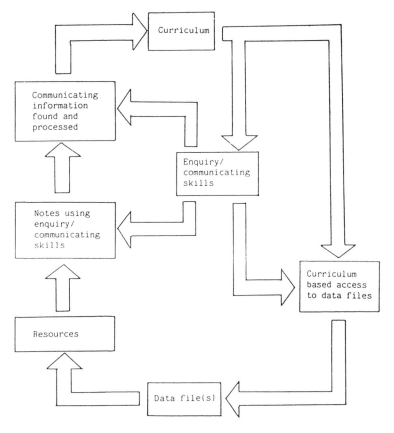

Fig. 6.4

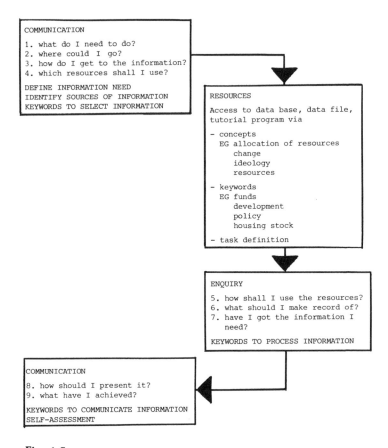

```
COMMUNICATION

1. what do I need to do?
2. where could I go?
3. how do I get to the information?
4. which resources shall I use?

DEFINE INFORMATION NEED
IDENTIFY SOURCES OF INFORMATION
KEYWORDS TO SELECT INFORMATION
```

```
RESOURCES

Access to data base, data file,
tutorial program via

- concepts
  EG allocation of resources
     change
     ideology
     resources
- keywords
  EG funds
     development
     policy
     housing stock
- task definition
```

```
ENQUIRY

5. how shall I use the resources?
6. what should I make record of?
7. have I got the information I
   need?

KEYWORDS TO PROCESS INFORMATION
```

```
COMMUNICATION

8. how should I present it?
9. what have I achieved?

KEYWORDS TO COMMUNICATE INFORMATION
SELF-ASSESSMENT
```

Fig. 6.5

Computerized information retrieval and information skills
In using the datafiles, pupils will be expected to use and extend the
following general categories of inquiry/communication skills

    selecting information   (communication skills)
    processing information   (inquiry skills)
    communicating information   (communication skills)

with the selecting and processing of information combining elements
of both inquiry and communication skills.

This 'information cycle' of selecting, processing and communicating information is designed to fit into the nine steps outlined
in *Information skills in the secondary curriculum*[7] and builds upon

previous information skills work done in the curriculum. This information cycle is shown in Figure 6.4 and, on the evidence of work done to date on the Housing Unit referred to earlier, this information cycle can be extended, as shown in Figure 6.5, which is part of the Housing Unit syllabus.

In helping pupils to use the microcomputer to retrieve information, either as a list of references or as statistics, the information skills set out in Figure 6.6 are learned as required.

The importance of concepts

The ability to assimilate information into concepts and to be aware of one's own learning process and capacity for transferring skills and information is seen to be an integral part of the information skills work done within the Modern Studies curriculum and indeed, all information skills work within the school in connection with information retrieval through the library systems.[8] This approach also forms the basis of the supporting information system and

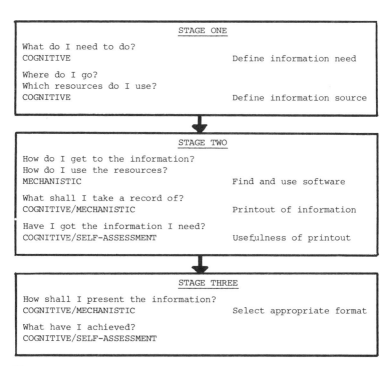

Fig. 6.6

successfully links both current educational philosophy and practice and school resources with learning opportunities.

In this context, a concept is regarded as a word which summarizes a regularly occurring process within the subjects taught in the Modern Studies syllabus. 'Cooperation', 'negotiation' and 'authority' are examples of curriculum-based concepts. These concepts also act as a 'way in' to a particular subject. A concept map becomes a focus point for thinking (conceptual skills) and a means of doing (manipulative and observational skills). It encompasses the central themes and interrelationships of lessons and units of work –

> A concept is a mental or cognitive representation of an object, idea or feeling. It is the building block for 'thinking'. It might be said we 'think' through concepts. Concepts are mental procedures by which we can create and recreate mental images of objects, ideas of feelings . . . They are capable of existing in different arrangements in different cognitive contexts . . . Concept maps are representations in a graphic form of the relationships between concepts.[9]

In the context of information skills and microcomputer information retrieval, a concept map becomes a .graphic representation of the relationships prevalent in the curriculum and the curriculum-based experiences of the pupils, showing the hierarchy, interrelationships and perceived orders of curriculum-based concepts.

Pupils are required to construct simple concept maps. This forms an effective revision medium, enabling the teacher to identify areas of difficulty and to quantify the assimilation of information in the pupil's own knowledge structures. These maps are an important vehicle for creativity and thought; grasping the interaction of context and conceptualization; and identifying the influence of perceptions and experiences on personal knowledge structures, in addition to reinforcing the process of concept categorization – the 'basic way in which humans impose order and meaning on the environment'.[10]

The information skills framework
Information skills in relation to computerized information retrieval are developed within the following framework

> information awareness and the information cycle of selecting, processing and communicating information
> computer awareness: the difference between databases and datafiles

Keywords are words which describe the ideas (themes) you find, and select, from information sources.

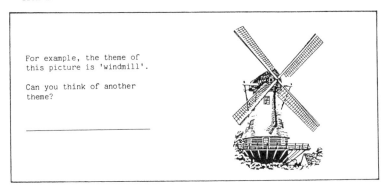

For example, the theme of this picture is 'windmill'.

Can you think of another theme?

Here is another picture. What do you think the themes are here?

Fig. 6.7

> information needs awareness: the articulation of purpose
> information source awareness: identifying, selecting and using relevant sources of information

which encompasses the multi-level cognitive skills of analysis, negotiation, interpretation and synthesis.

Some of the material for this framework was developed from work done on an earlier pupil-created datafile project. An example of this work is shown in Figure 6.7.

The value of computerized information retrieval lies not only in the in-depth storage and retrieval of information but in the opportunity for developing in-depth search strategies free from the restraints of searching a number of bibliographic tools for relevant information. The Modern Studies data files contain references to all media in the library – including periodical articles, video programmes, books and newspaper cuttings, so all pupils are required to make only one search for information. This releases more time within the inquiry unit allocation for the development of such information skills as note taking and, in particular, the important first step: defining a need for information.

Defining information needs and the concept/keyword maps

Both the school librarian and the teacher view information skills as an integral part of the content and process of the Modern Studies syllabus. The concept/keyword map forms the centre of activity for information retrieval, providing both a reinforcement of the content of the syllabus and an opportunity to develop skills in the process of defining information needs.

The teacher encourages pupils to consider information in the context of De Bono's *PMI – Plus, Minus and Interesting.*[11] When pupils are aware of this process, the design of concept maps, with their hierarchical arrays and interrelated groups, forms first a natural extension and then an eventual integration with the information

China :– Communes : Reform > Economy–Government

Fig. 6.8

handling process, whether done in the class or in inquiry work in the library.

Figure 6.8 shows a reproduction of a concept map developed by second-year pupils (aged 12-13) as part of their Alternative Ideologies unit work. This map was produced in class following pupil-teacher discussion and then used by the author to produce the required keyword access to the Alternative Ideologies datafile.

This type of work avoids the issue of providing synonym access to information stored in the microcomputer – a problem heightened by the increased access to information through keywords and a release from the restraints of card-based subject indexes and catalogues. Pupils *know* which keywords to use to find information since the keywords are part of their classwork and this helps to prevent lengthy and potentially confusing *or* searches designed to solve the problems of synonyms.

The use of Boolean logic when using the microcomputer for information retrieval was highlighted by the SIR project[12] and can be difficult for pupils. Boolean logic introduces pupils to the combination of keywords using AND, OR and NOT – e.g. PARLIAMENT AND FINANCE OR LAWS – would retrieve references to books, articles etc. which were indexed under PARLIAMENT and FINANCE or PARLIAMENT and LAWS. The teacher and the author have experimented with games to introduce pupils to Boolean logic by using the examples of combinations of colours but pupils have regarded these as too juvenile. Another approach being considered is to allow pupils to develop this information skill as they go through inquiry work. Use of the microcomputer is seen as part of the syllabus, so skill reinforcement and development is assured and, as is well known, the best kind of learning occurs when pupils are doing work which they regard as useful.

The program being used is KWIRS2 which allows the pupils to search for information using Boolean logic. The microcomputer asks pupils to enter a keyword and then displays the number of 'hits' i.e. how many entries have been indexed using that keyword. Pupils then have to choose to combine keywords using AND, OR or NOT and enter a second keyword. The microcomputer then searches the file to discover any entries indexed using both keywords.

Using the system
Information skills such as concept/keyword analysis do not depend on the type of microcomputer program used and thus little time is spent on teaching skills based on the technical aspects of using the microcomputer. Pupils can produce valuable work without being

sophisticated users of the system. Pupils develop skills and confidence in operating the microcomputer e.g. loading software, through use and by cooperating with each other in the use of the system.

The emphasis at Milne's High School is on the development of the interrelated keyword skills and information need definition. Handling the information held in the system is more important than handling the system, for the system is merely a means to an end. Experience has shown that pupils readily learn system handling skills.

Transferability is emphasized and pupils are encouraged to view concept/keyword maps as evolving access routes to the information contained within the system and, as shown above, they can themselves be proactive rather than passive users when they define concept/keyword maps for the librarian to index resources from. In the school context, the information skills and computerized information retrieval are an integral part of the syllabus, reinforcing and being reinforced by the syllabus units. There becomes little need for separate information skills programmes when integration is complete. Each part of the content and process becomes interrelated in the use of the system.

The Housing Unit Group
Figure 6.9 shows the EDFAX-based design of one page from the Housing Unit database. It is intended that all the information will be presented in a graphical, rather than tabular form and that, where relevant, concept/keyword maps will be inserted as part of the access to the information. This, combined with external concept/keyword access – through either maps or the Housing Unit datafile – will help pupils identify the true relationships between topics, which may not be so clear using a program such as EDFAX. This is an important area for school librarians and teachers to consider about the design and layout of information held on the microcomputer in relation to the identification of curriculum-related keywords and the development of information skills.

The basic principles of defining information needs and using concepts and keywords to access information via the microcomputer are also being integrated into the work of the Housing Unit Group. A major part of the Unit involves inquiry work where pupils are required to manipulate information retrieved from a database and then reproduce that information through a program containing such graphical options such as bar charts and pie charts.

As part of this process, the pupils will develop such information skills as

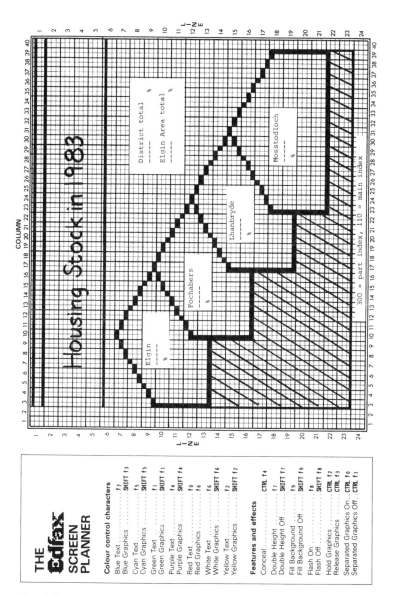

Fig. 6.9

75

interpreting and synthesizing information and its sources
criticizing and evaluating their work

through the process outlined in Figure 6.5 above.

HOUSING UNIT - PART ONE

Activity Sheet

1.   Use the computer to make a comparison
      of private housing in Elgin and
      Fochabers

Pupil checklist

I need information on -
(tick)

Private housing
Public housing
Elgin
Fochabers
Lhanbryde
Mosstodloch

Arranged as

A pie chart
A table
A map
A silhouette
Blocks

I need to -
(tick)

Load
'Key concepts'
'Housing Stock'

Get a printout of -

Housing stock
Information needed

Fig. 6.10

Problems requiring information are given to pupils both as individuals and as members of groups and formative evaluation, both by teachers and pupils, of their inquiry/communication skills will be an integral part of the Unit. Problems may vary from small, well-defined needs for information to larger issues requiring more detailed awareness and manipulation of concepts and information. An example of how a pupil-based inquiry may develop is shown in the Activity Sheet in Figure 6.10.

Conclusion

The opening quotation for this chapter should be placed over every school library catalogue for the message is the need for librarians to provide learners with a means for learning about the interrelationships of subjects in an increasingly multi-disciplinary school environment. The same holds true for microcomputer-based information retrieval systems, where users can avoid the frustrating and depressing array of *see* references which appear in card-based retrieval systems. Using curriculum-based access can simplify the problem of synonyms and remove this inhibition from information system users.

It may be considererd that there is little in the way of information skills worksheets or programmes at Milne's High School. Pupils learn by doing and by evaluating the effectiveness of what they have done. By reducing the need to handle a complicated system, time is released from the already tight schedules for pupils to develop skills through a process whereby creative association and opportunities to learn and think are highly valued.

Arguably, the information skills shown in this chapter may have been associated with manual retrieval systems. They are transferable and pupils should be encouraged to create keyword maps as part of any information handling situation – even exam revision. The arrival of microcomputer-based information retrieval systems such as KWIRS and SIR has focused attention on the importance of information skills. The microcomputer is a means to an end and it provides an opportunity for developing search strategies because it is a unique storage medium which releases time for more cognitive skills within the information cycle of selecting, processing and communicating information and it is these educational skills which are valued by teachers and librarians.

References
1. Wall, J. D., 'Libraries as resources in schools,' *School Librarian*, 22(4), June 1974, 125.

2. Gilman, J. A., 'The resourcerer's apprentice,' *Education Libraries Bulletin*, 25(3), Autumn 1982, 3.
3. Department of Education and Science, *Microelectronics Education Programme, the strategy*, HMSO, 1981.
4. Davison, S., 'Data file creation – a case study,' *Education Libraries Bulletin*, 27(3), Autumn 1984, 52–8.
5. Mr J. Wilkie, Aberdeen College of Education.
6. Scottish Education Department, *Standard Grade Modern Studies*, SED, 1984.
7. Marland, M. ed., *Information skills in the secondary curriculum*, Methuen, 1981.
8. See for example, Malone, J. and Dekkers, J., 'The concept map as an aid to instruction in science and mathematics,' *School Science and Mathematics*, 84(3), March 1984, 220–31.
9. McAleese, R., 'Some problems of knowledge representation in an authoring environment,' *PLET*, 22(4), 1985, 304.
10. Farb, P., *Human kind*, Cape, 1978, 322.
11. See for example, *De Bono's Thinking Course*, BBC, 1982.
12. Rowbottom, M. *et al.*, *Schools Information Retrieval (SIR) Project*, British Library, 1983.

Chapter 7
Prestel in the school library
by Jan Condon

' . . . the quality of school work can be improved where LEAs and schools succeed in making available to both primary and secondary pupils an adequate stock of books and other information (*including new technology*) through the school library.'[1]

One area where the school librarian can contribute to the development of new technology in the school is the use of viewdata systems. The first part of this chapter will provide a definition of Prestel, the best known viewdata in the UK, give some background information, some of the reasons why school librarians should be concerned with Prestel and some of the questions raised through this involvement.

What is Prestel?
Prestel is the name given to the public viewdata system developed in the UK by the Post Office Research Laboratories in the 1970s. Prestel was launched in 1979 to provide users with instant access to thousands of pages of information and the ability to communicate with other Prestel users and with some of those who provided information for the system.[2]

The technology differs fundamentally from the more domestically familiar teletext systems, Ceefax and Oracle (see Figure 7.1).[3] Teletext uses a broadcast signal to communicate information to specially adapted television sets, while Prestel uses a telephone link to allow access to information. The user can gain access through a viewdata terminal or a microcomputer with the appropriate software and a modem, which allows the microcomputer to be used as a terminal. The differences in technology also mean that teletext is slower, has a smaller capacity and is less interactive than Prestel. Another major difference is in the originators of the information. While teletext is produced by television companies, Prestel information comes from a wide variety of sources – government, commercial and educational, known collectively as Information Providers (IPs).

That Prestel has an educational potential was recognized and in 1982, a joint initiative was launched by CET, British Telecom and the

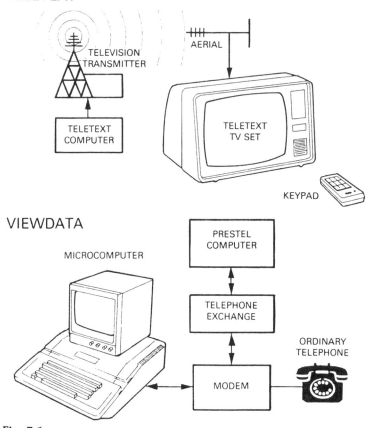

TELETEXT

VIEWDATA

Fig. 7.1

Department of Trade and Industry. The Prestel in Schools project[4] identified six objectives:

1. to educate young people in information technology
2. to show that Prestel is a general information source
3. to provide a cheap means of obtaining telesoftware
4. to provide Prestel to schools at a low introductory cost
5. to aid British industry in I.T. 82 Year
6. to educate teachers in the new technology both as an information source and teaching aid.

In addition, there were local initiatives such as Club 403 which attempted to provide viewdata to domestic consumers in a limited geographical area. The educational project within Club 403 aimed to investigate what education could offer a residential viewdata service and to discover what use might be made of Prestel in schools and colleges.[5] Market research had suggested that there was a role for viewdata in education and it was with this project that Solihull Sixth Form College (SSFC) became involved.

The Prestel Education scheme, launched by CET and British Telecom provided all schools with the means to turn their microcomputers into Prestel terminals with the offer of software and modem to allow communication. In March 1986, a special offer for school librarians was issued, giving low cost access to Prestel for a limited period.[6]

What can Prestel offer the school library?
In the school library, Prestel can be seen as part of the total information and learning environment. What it can offer will be illustrated in case studies below, but can be summed up as

- a general information carrier, providing instant access to a variety of information which is more up to date than printed sources
- an educational service, providing information on new technology, higher education, careers, educational developments and new educational products
- a gateway service, providing access to remote databases such as ECCTIS (see below)
- a service providing access to other viewdata systems via Bulletin (W.M.), Monitel
- a mailbox facility, allowing electronic communication between schools and other users and providing contact points for school librarians and teachers
- a software service providing telesoftware[7] and enabling users to obtain access to software via Prestel Education and Micronet
- a microviewdata service, allowing users to create their own databases through Prestel

Why school librarians should consider Prestel
Tom Stonier, in *Wealth of information* gives a neat and explicit reason for educating young people in the uses of new technology, when he states, 'An educated workforce learns how to exploit new technology; an ignorant one becomes its victim'.[8] It could also be said that this quotation applies to school librarians, as part of the

educational workforce. The reasons for school librarians becoming involved with Prestel, in the context of pupil learning and working with subject teachers include:

The 'Mount Everest' syndrome
Prestel as a challenge because it is there. The school librarian, unlike most professional librarians works alone, usually the only professional librarian in the school. There is, therefore, a heavy responsibility to be professionally concerned with all potential information and learning media and to be able to inform colleagues and advise on and assess the potential use and/or value of such media.

There is a need
A need exists to provide pupils with the opportunity to use viewdata systems as part of their general education and to show pupils how to use viewdata critically. A need also exists to demonstrate to pupils new ways of finding information and assessing the quality of information they can obtain from Prestel. Teachers also need help and advice in the curricular use of Prestel, via the school library and this may involve the school librarian in in-service training in the school.

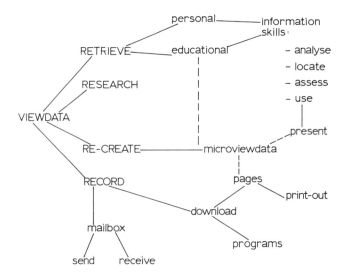

Fig. 7.2

The information environment
The school library is a major part of the information environment in the school and the school librarian, in her/his neutral position, can ensure that Prestel is used across the curriculum and not only in one subject area.

The CET Educational Viewdata User Guide pack[9] gives a sound introduction to Prestel in schools. Section 1.5 is especially useful for relating information technology and information skills and their importance in the curriculum. The case studies which follow will attempt to highlight the skills cited by CET. These include information, life, study and library skills and the additional cognitive and manual skills needed to use technology to handle information.

The three Rs
Three main uses for viewdata can be identified. As figure 7.2 shows, all are interrelated in the demands they make on pupils.

Retrieval – finding quick reference-type information for personal needs e.g. times of trains, theatre information, higher education information.
Research – finding information to be incorporated into assignments, projects and topics. Research can be technology-led (contrived use of viewdata in the curriculum) or information-led (spontaneous use of viewdata to answer questions or solve problems).
Re-creation – using microviewdata/viewdata to compile, synthesize (and therefore re-create) in-house databases, which may be based on original research or other forms of information, including information from viewdata sources.

In addition, a fourth R could be cited, as Recording, referring to the facility to download software or pages to disk for off-line use and the ability to send and receive electronic mail.

Case study 1: Solihull Sixth Form College (SSFC) (see Figure 7.3)
Prestel was installed in the library under the Club 403 scheme in 1983 and is accessed via an alphanumeric keyboard and viewdata television. Solihull LEA have supported Prestel Education in the college for the last year.
Prestel can now be accessed through the set or via a microcomputer and modem located beside it in the Community Information section in the library. It was decided to keep the

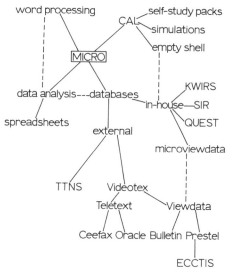

Fig. 7.3

viewdata set to allow ease of access and also because of heavy use of
the microcomputers in the library. Under Club 403, Prestel was used
very much for retrieval and for research. Prestel is seen very much as
part of the total library resources and current use is demonstrated
below in the three areas identified.

1. Retrieval
Query: How easy is it to get to Mull?
Students, who were local Venture Scouts, had a specific information
need. To solve their problem, they had to locate and use an O.S. map
in the library; decide what form of transport they would use; locate
and use a B.R. map to find the nearest station; and find the name of
the nearest town likely to have a bus station. They then had to use
Prestel to make comparisons between the methods of transport in
terms of cost, time taken and ease of access.

Query: I want to do English as a subject at a polytechnic and would
like to do something to do with Ancient Greek culture as well. The
polytechnic handbook which I used was not much help and my tutor
has told me to ask the librarian for help.
   The background to this inquiry was that with the introduction of
'gateway' facilities on Prestel – the ability to use another database by

Please answer these questions before making your search.
You will need this information as a starting point.
You can amend your search on-line.

```
┌─────────────────────────────────────────────────────────────┐
│ FRAME 1 (Please circle)                                       │
├───────────────────────────────┬───────────────────────────────┤
│ 1. Level of course            │ 2. Method of study            │
│                               │                               │
│ A Postgraduate                │ A Full time                   │
│ B Teaching*                   │ B Sandwich                    │
│   First degree                │ C Part time                   │
│ C Single subjects             │ D Home study                  │
│ D Combined                    │ E In-service                  │
│ E Teaching*                   │                               │
│ F Advanced                    │ ++Any                         │
│ G Non advanced                │                               │
│                               │                               │
│ *PGCE/B Ed                    │                               │
├───────────────────────────────┴───────────────────────────────┤
│ 3. Place of study                                             │
│                                                               │
│ ++ All                          H W Midlands                  │
│ A England                       I E Midlands                  │
│ B N Ireland                     J E Anglia                    │
│ C Scotland                      K Home counties               │
│ D Wales                         L London                      │
│ E N England                     M SW England                  │
│ F NW England                    N SE England                  │
│ G Yorkshire/Humberside          P More specific               │
│                                                               │
├─────────────────────────────────────────────────────────────┤
│ FRAME 2                                                       │
├─────────────────────────────────────────────────────────────┤
│ 1. (please circle)                                            │
│ u University                    c College                     │
│ p Polytechnic                   ++Any                         │
├─────────────────────────────────────────────────────────────┤
│ 2. Subjects                                                   │
│                                                               │
│ 1. ......................                                     │
│ 2. ......................                                     │
│ 3. ......................                                     │
├─────────────────────────────────────────────────────────────┤
│ Date ......................                                   │
│ Time on ...................                                   │
│ Computer D/R ............... (please circle)                  │
│ Time off ..................                                   │
└─────────────────────────────────────────────────────────────┘
```

ECCTIS
Educational Counselling and
Credit Transfer Service.

Fig. 7.4

Name...	PRESTEL ENQUIRY VOUCHER
Tutor set..Staff................	
Subjects.................................... .... Pages.................	
of	
enquiry...	
....	

Office use

Time on .... Time off ....

Rate................................ Computer

called...................................

Charges............................

Comments of user..

Fig. 7.5

means of Prestel – the library could gain access to ECCTIS, a higher education database. All tutors were circulated with an information handout on ECCTIS and notices were put in the daily bulletin.

To solve the problem, the student had to: think carefully about what course she wanted; decide on keywords to key into ECCTIS by using the ECCTIS index; negotiate with the librarian on terminology use; commit the parameters of the inquiry to a form (see Figure 7.4); and use the Prestel gateway. The result of this inquiry was four possible courses which the student followed up by reference to individual prospectus and discussion with her tutor.

SSFC library has an inquiry voucher (see Figure 7.5) for all Prestel uses. This encourages students to think out their information needs first. They then check the printed index first, to save telephone time, note the page numbers they wish to start at and then ask a member of the library staff for a line to Prestel. They are given brief instructions on moving around the system and there is a guide to page changing next to the set.

2. Research
Query: I want to find out something about smoking.
The background to this inquiry was that all students doing social studies as a supplementary study have to produce a project which is assessed by Birmingham Polytechnic. They are given advice on choosing topics by their tutors, the librarian talks to them about the skills they will need (based on the nine steps approach)[10] and the

```
PRESTEL                    1621a
Medical advice

BRITISH ORGAN DONOR SOCIETY
Help and advice, cards and donations

HEALTH EDUCATION COUNCIL
Smoking food and fitness, immunisation,
family planning. Free publications via
Prestel

DHSS Health and travelling abroad -
medical costs, insurance and precautions

PRESTEL ADVERTISER - MEDICAL ADVICE
 CHILD CARE
VACCINATION
CONTRACEPTION AND PREGNANCY
HEALTH
```

```
HEC HEALTH EDUCATION       54417513a


ASH    Effects of smoking on health

In the United Kingdom at least 100,000
people are killed by smoking each year.
It has been estimated that out of 1000
young men in the UK who smoke, 1 will be
murdered, 6 will die in road accidents
and 250 will die prematurely as a result
of their smoking.

It has been estimated that 50 million
working days a year are lost through
illness caused by smoking.  Surveys show
that smokers of 20 cigarettes or more a
day have twice as much time off work as
do non-smokers.

1 more statistics     9  index
```

Fig. 7.6

range of information available. The librarian also offers an information consultancy where students can arrange a time to seek advice on information aspects of the project.

This student had to:

- define the parameters of the subject
- use the library subject index
- locate a range of materials – cassettes, topic folders, books
- learn to use Clover Index[11] to trace periodical literature
- check Prestel for any up-to-the-minute information
- send for materials through the Mailbox facility

The library provided a print-out of the HEC/ASH pages the student selected (see Figure 7.6). The inquirer could not print out the pages herself at this point as the microcomputer was in use, so they were printed out and passed on to her. As this subject could well come up again during the current academic year, the pages were downloaded on to disk, so that they could be consulted off-line without incurring further expense.

Query: What has the library got on race and immigration?

The last two weeks of the college year are given over to work experience or end of year activities (EYA). The latter comprises courses which can be taken at varying times throughout the fortnight. One of the courses was concerned with a range of social issues and was designed to encourage the students to think about their own attitudes. The teacher running the course checked out materials in the library as part of her planning for the course. She located most of the resources but checked with the librarian to see if there was anything 'in the pipeline' which could be added to what she already had. When asked about statistical material, the teacher stated that she had the national statistics. The librarian then directed her to the West Midlands Bulletin (see Figure 7.7), the private viewdata service which can be accessed via Prestel equipment. The teacher scanned the information available and later asked to use the library for the class.

The teacher thus:

- added to the information she already had
- became aware of a different information source
- learned how to use that source
- used the source to present information in a different way

and the class:

WM County

WMCC
CENSUS
DATA

key no to see Census Data for area

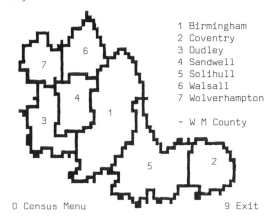

1 Birmingham
2 Coventry
3 Dudley
4 Sandwell
5 Solihull
6 Walsall
7 Wolverhampton

- W M County

0 Census Menu   9 Exit

B U L L E T I N   CENSUS 1981   0p

Profile of

Key Statistics

WMCC
CENSUS
DATA

SOLIHULL DISTRICT

	1971	1981	% Change
Population	192071	199261	3.7
Males	94472	97904	3.6
Females	97596	101357	3.9
Pensioners	19752	27289	38.2
% Econ Active	50.2%	65.0%	14.8
% Unemployed	3.8%	9.0%	5.2
Households	61619	69825	13.3
One person households	6969	11612	67.6
Houses & Flats	61945	71389	15.2
No Overcrowded	2608	1983	-24.0
No Lacking WC	1249	373	-70.1

1 Help 2 More 3 Change Area 9 Exit

89

- also became aware of the information source
- responded actively to the on-screen presentation of statistical material
- could all use the material at the same time
- manipulated the material easily, moving to and from different parts of the database as they thought appropriate to support their arguments

The viewdata presentation therefore:

- allowed ease of display and manipulation of information in a way in which a chalkboard, flip chart or handout could not and became a kind of electronic chalkboard
- provided a catalyst for discussion of subject matter
- related easily the subject matter to the students' own geographical and social environment
- encouraged the development of oral discussion based on evidence inferred from information rather than expressed, but unsupported, opinion

Contrived: travel information

Information by and for the travel industry is a major area in Prestel and one which can be readily exploited by school librarians and teachers for curricular and personal use. A number of students in SSFC carry out work experience in the travel industry each year. One student had been asked if she had used Prestel before and as she had not, the librarian, consulting with the Borough Careers Officer attached to the college and the head of External Services who arranges placements, devised three short problem-solving exercises which simulated real inquiries. There is now a training pack for the trade[12] but these in-house materials provided some pre-vocational experience for students who might be interested. The exercises are being piloted by a small number of students with a view to presenting a short course or self-study package later this year.

The students had to

- analyse a fairly complex series of inquiries
- plan an information search
- scan, read and interpret tabulated information
- provide answers to 'real life' questions
- decide on suitable alternatives e.g. on suitable flights for clients

In this exercise, the library is providing a service to meet an expressed need; there is active cooperation with other professional

90

EN VACANCES
(OU ON PEUT TROUVER L'INFORMATION)

Your family has decided to buy your parents
a holiday in France as a wedding present.
The parents have chosen a few days in Paris.
They would like to travel on Friday or
Saturday and return home midweek.
   A good hotel and travel preferably from
Birmingham would be ideal.
   1. Using Prestel, find a hotel in Paris
which you think would be suitable. Give as
many details as possible e.g. types of room,
tariffs etc.
   2. Using the word processor, write to the
hotel asking for accommodation.
   3. Plan the journey by air, land and sea,
in case the threatened baggage handlers dis-
pute materialises.
   Prestel hint: start by looking up the
number for France in the Prestel Directory.

```
                                        344201a
FRENCH NATIONAL TOURIST OFFICE

PARIS AND THE REGIONS OF FRANCE

01 Paris/Ile de France
02 Alsace Vosges Lorraine
03 Aquitaine
04 Auvergne
05 Brittany
06 Burgundy
07 Champagne Ardenne
08 Corsica
09 Dauphiny Alps
10 Franche Comte
11 Languedoc Roussillon
12 Limousin
13 Loire Valley (Centre)
14 Midi Pyrenees
```

Fig. 7.8

staff in the school; and staff are introduced to the potential of information technology.

En vacances (see Figure 7.8)

The head of modern language in the college has introduced the Intermediate French course designed by York University. The aims of the course are essentially practical and the skills to be developed are concerned with language use in the context of life skills. The teacher was aware of Prestel and word processing and had previously discussed with the librarian possible uses by her department. Although Prestel is a British database, it was agreed that it could be used to provide real information for part of the course work. 'En vacances' was a short exercise which involved the location of information and incorporating some of it into a letter to be written in French, using a word processor. A small group of students worked out their search strategy to find the information on Prestel and the exercise proved popular and successful. This exercise will be incorporated in the course next year and the teacher and librarian are preparing material for TVEI modules next year.

In this exercise, students were:

- introduced to Prestel as an integral part of their course
- introduced to Prestel in the context of information technology –
  using the word processing package
- relating the exercise to a real situation
- planning how to find information
- involved in scanning and interpreting information

The library was again cooperating with a teacher in planning the exercise; demonstrating a new source of information to students; enabling students who might not otherwise do so, to use new technology in a way which is related to their curricular and personal needs.

3. Re-creation

A small project was set up with a group of students who had chosen library work as part of their Foundation Study. The librarian had to carefully plan aspects of the project, in which the students would create their own information database on local pubs and clubs using the MICROVIEWDATA software, to cover aspects such as the involvement of other staff, the amount of supervision needed by students, the appropriateness of using the software for this kind of information i.e. was the project information-led or technology-led?

The students (all over 18 years of age) chose a topic of interest to

```
MEP SOFTWARE        122a        Op

    THE SHIRLEY WINE BAR:

    227 Stratford Road
        Shirley
            Solihull.

Opening times

10am-4pm coffee bar

12pm-2.30pm bar

7pm-10.30pm bar
     11pm Fri and Sat

Food

Cakes and pastries - coffee bar

Hot and cold lunches
e.g. lasagne, scampi, pies

Special offers
Promotion nights
            KEY * to cont
```

Fig. 7.9

themselves and of potential use to others. The students' aim was to produce a database and they were thus involved in skills of defining their information needs, planning methods of acquiring information, and assessing the information needs of the users of the database. Other skills involved were the planning of time, the allocation of tasks, drawing up a questionnaire to be used to cover local facilities, telephoning and interviewing local licensees and decision-making in relation to the selection, organization and editing of information gathered.

As well as doing original research, the students used a wide range of library materials to support their work. Prestel was used for ideas on screen presentation and demonstration materials were used off-line and on-line. The students used a word processing program for the questionnaire. Local telephone directories, A-Z street maps, local guides and dictionaries all proved invaluable.

In terms of educational skills, the process of planning for and collection of the information were most important. A strong motivational aspect, highlighted by many school librarians and teachers, was the fact that students were creating an original database which would be used by other students. Figure 7.9 shows a print-out from one page of the database which other students found informative and very easy to use.

The benefits to the library of such projects can be seen in terms of increased relevance to the curriculum, the creation of original information sources by students and in terms of the image of the library.

Case study 2: The Holgate school
The Holgate school is a split-site comprehensive in Hucknall, Nottinghamshire. Information skills curricula have been developed for pupils throughout the school and are closely linked to the use of new technology. The librarian has developed some excellent information skills software packages[13] which are used in cooperation with other school staff on a variety of projects. Prestel is located in the Middle School library at present and is used primarily for retrieval and research work. Demonstrations of Prestel are given as part of the information skills courses and pupils have the opportunity to try out the system. Demonstrations are also given to staff and to sixth formers with an emphasis on careers and higher education information. The following examples of work illustrate how viewdata is being integrated into the work of the library and the school.

1. Retrieval
Query: I want to know about the nearest sports centre and the types of sport which go on there.

This pupil had seen Prestel demonstrated as part of the information skills programme. A keen player of games at school, he was interested in finding out what local facilities offered in terms of learning and practising new sports in the holidays. The inquiry represents a genuine need for information which could have been partly fulfilled by traditional means such as telephone books or local guides but which could be investigated more thoroughly by using Prestel. The librarian wishes pupils to learn to use the whole system on-line and encourages pupils to use indexes on screen in preference to the printed version.

To find the information, the pupil had to:

– define exactly what he wanted to know

- decide how far he was able to travel to get to a sports centre
- find out the opening hours, which sports he was interested in and the cost of using the facilities

The information on the Sports Council database helped the pupil to clarify his real needs for information and make decisions based on the information he found. A sample page is shown in Figure 7.10.

Query: What qualifications do I need to become a stunt-man?

This inquiry was from a third-year pupil who had seen Prestel demonstrated in the information skills course where there is an emphasis on career information and the pupils use the large collection of career materials in the library.

The pupil checked relevant sources in the library and used Prestel on-line to access the database on careers provided by COIC. He did not find the relevant information, but was able to use the Prestel mailbox facility to send a message to COIC. Within two days, the pupil received a reply via Mailbox, informing him that he would need acting experience and an Equity card.

Prestel has developed quite definite strengths in the area of careers and higher education (see ECCTIS above). Not only can information which may take considerable time to locate but which needs to be as up-to-date as possible be handled by Prestel but the ability to communicate personal, one-off inquiries to the information providers is a great advantage. As the system allows the information to be updated easily, it can provide an important service to those applying for jobs or places in higher education. For example, the Polytel database indicates which courses are full or have vacancies.

The careers and higher education information is dynamic, interactive, specialist, comprehensive and time-saving and an excellent aid to school staff whose time is at a premium. It provides access to information, the currency of which is not in doubt, something which cannot be true of printed guides.

2. Research

Query: Second-year pupils are seeking information on what their food contains.

The pupils were to pay special attention to vitamins and had been asked to find out what the 'E' numbers mean on prepared foods. All pupils had seen Prestel demonstrated in their information skills course. As this kind of inquiry is well provided for by the Ministry of Agriculture, Fisheries and Food database, it gave the librarian a chance to have pupils use this source of information to support their project work.

```
SPORTS COUNCIL                    30071a
   EAST MIDLAND REGION


1 Sports centres in the region
2 Publications from the Regional Sports Council
3 Events in the region
4 Ice rinks
5 Sports injury clinics

For further information on sport and recreation
in:
Derbyshire, Leicestershire, Lincolnshire
Northamptonshire, Nottinghamshire contact:

Sports Council (East Midland Region)
26 Musters Rd, West Bridgford, Nottingham
NG2 7PL
Tel: Nottingham 821887/822586


   Key 8 for Regional index
   Key 9 for Main index
```

Sports

```
SPORTS COUNCIL                    300114d
   COMMUNITY SPORTS CENTRES AND HALLS
   EAST MIDLAND REGION - NOTTINGHAMSHIRE

Hucknall Leisure Centre, Linby Rd, Hucknall,
Nottingham. Tel: 640461.

Huthwaite Leisure Centre, New St, Huthwaite,
Mansfield. Tel: 0623 550076

John Carroll Leisure Centre, Denman St,
Off Ilkeston Rd, Nottingham.
Tel: Nottingham 780061

Kissingate Centre, Park Rd, Shirebrook,
Mansfield, Notts.
Tel: 0623 748313

Key - to continue
Key 0 for EM Sports Centres index
```

Fig. 7.10

Pupils were expected to analyse their inquiries; check Prestel on-line; locate, scan and extract information from the tables on screen; and incorporate this information into their project. With a careful introduction to the database, pupils were made aware that the information they had access to was the same information available to those in the food and catering industry and to consumer groups. Thus they were using important, 'real world' information for their project but they might well use the same source and information later in this adult lives.

Query: The teacher of first-year humanities was seeking information on the Australian aborigines. He had checked the range of materials available in the library but wanted pupils to do some research in the library for the project. The librarian suggested that tourist information provided on Prestel might be usefully looked at. The teacher also wanted the class to produce project files which were illustrated.

While Aborigines may not appear an obvious choice of topic for a viewdata search, the teacher nevertheless found that the tourist information on Australia not only provided some useful background material, but could be used to obtain travel brochures in quantity, which the pupils could then use as a visual source. The class came into the library and were involved in a Prestel search. The class also used the Mailbox facility to ask for brochures which were sent to the school.

In this inquiry, the teacher added to the information available; became aware of the different possibilities of viewdata; learned how to exploit viewdata; and provided the class with an interesting and lively activity.

The class were able to use a new information source; to locate and extract information from that source; use Mailbox to send for further information; see tangible results from their Mailbox request; and obtained up-to-date and vivid information which would have been hard to get from another source. Figure 7.11 shows part of the Prestel search done by the class.

The fourth 'R' – recording
The flexibility of Prestel as a means of the communication of information is considerable. The two-way, interactive nature of Prestel has been shown above in the case studies where the Mailbox facilities were used to obtain information and learning materials.

Other communications or recording aspects are provided by the terminal emulator software and these are becoming increasingly important.

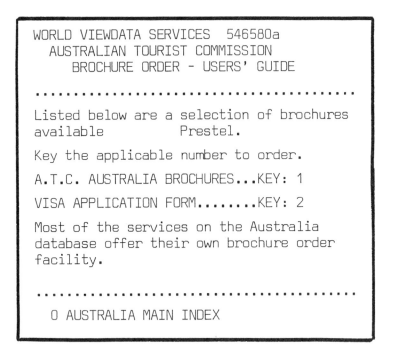

```
WORLD VIEWDATA SERVICES  546580a
   AUSTRALIAN TOURIST COMMISSION
     BROCHURE ORDER - USERS' GUIDE

.........................................

Listed below are a selection of brochures
available          Prestel.

Key the applicable number to order.

A.T.C. AUSTRALIA BROCHURES...KEY: 1

VISA APPLICATION FORM........KEY: 2

Most of the services on the Australia
database offer their own brochure order
facility.


.........................................

   0 AUSTRALIA MAIN INDEX
```

Fig. 7.11

downloading software

Both the Holgate School and Solihull SFC have started to scan regularly the software pages as both libraries have a policy to provide information on and, where appropriate, software materials in the library. Prestel Education started its own software service in the Autumn term of 1985 and feedback so far suggests that this is a service which schools find most welcome. Packages are well described, prices given before the user is invited to download i.e. transfer the programs on to the users' own disk. Charges made for programs vary but are generally well below retail costs. Some material is a 'taster' service and a complete package can be ordered from the software producer separately. Documentation is sent through the post when software is downloaded. This is a developing service which should also develop software standards in the future. Computer software, as Chapter 8 demonstrates, now has a permanent place in the school library and using Prestel allows the school librarian with a chance to get started.

* *downloading pages*

Pages of information can also be downloaded and used off-line. Reasons for wanting to do this may not be restricted to cost, although for many this will be the most important factor. Other reasons are that Prestel pages can be included in microviewdata bases alongside pages created by pupils; Prestel pages on a specific subject can be downloaded to disk and the disk incorporated into an information package, with slides, tapes and printed materials; and that Prestel may not always be available in the place where the information is needed, thus downloading allows for flexibility in that, for example, pages of graphics can be used for work in the art department.

Conclusion

'Will your children go to school?' asks an IBM poster. Tom Stonier has envisaged a scenario where children learn at home, guided by technology and grandparents and go to school for socialization.[14] Whether or not schools as we know them will exist in the future is uncertain but we can be sure that there will be information and that its importance will grow in social and economic terms.

The Information Technology Advisory Panel stated that

> The users of the future may well be more informationally competent than today's users but will have to deal with orders of magnitude increasing in environmental complexity. If competence and complexity are increasing correlatively, tomorrow's user will be in a sense no better off than his present day counterpart. That being the case, the users of the future will continue to turn to intermediaries, information specialists, for guidance and help.[15]

School librarians can help their users to prepare for the complexities of the future and using viewdata in the school library can provide an introduction to the concepts of organization and interrogation of information which will play a part in the future working and domestic lives of today's pupils. Schools already have access to Prestel and other hosts using the same equipment. Currently, NERIS, the National Educational Resource Information Service from the Department of Trade and Industry is being planned. In addition to teaching pupils and teachers how to use these sources of information, school librarians will be needed to help users to choose the appropriate sources, expanding the traditional role of intermediary to that of information manager and emphasizing the place of the school librarian as an educator.

References
1. Department of Education and Science, *Better schools*, HMSO, 1985.
2. McKee, R., *The information age*, Forbes Pubs., 1985.
3. Burton, J. and Taylor, J., *Educational viewdata user guide*, CET, 1985.
4. Owen, K. ed., *Videotex in education*, CET, 1982.
5. McKee, R., 'Education: the way ahead', *Club 403 Magazine*, (2), August 1984.
6. Prestel Education booklet, British Telecom, 1986.
7. Knowles, C. and Bell, C., *Distribution of educational software through Prestel*, CET, 1984.
8. Stonier, T., *The wealth of information*, Methuen, 1983.
9. Burton and Taylor, *op. cit.*
10. Marland, M. ed., *Information skills in the secondary curriculum*, Methuen, 1981.
11. Clover Index available from M. Woodrow, 8 Ashby Drive, Biggleswade, Beds.
12. *CET News*, (25), January 1986.
13. Schmidt File and Information Skills packages.
14. Stonier, *op. cit.*
15. Information Technology Advisory Panel, *Making a business of information*, HMSO, 1983.

Chapter 8
Criteria for selecting software
by Judith Askey

Introduction
The task of selecting software is largely subjective. There is no
established set of criteria. The field of educational computing is still
in its infancy and changing rapidly. We can expect, in the next
decade, to see more sophisticated hardware and software produced
as users become more expert and practised in the best ways of using
computers in the learning process.

The first question which should be asked on this subject is – why
use microcomputers? Is the starting point for the selection of
software either (a) because in this technological era everyone should
know about microcomputers or (b) for sound learning aims and
objectives? i.e. do school librarians and teachers start from the skills
and processes or because of the existence of software? It is only in the
context of the answers to these questions that relevant and helpful
criteria for selection can be developed.

Primary considerations in the selection of software

The six question steps
1) What skills and concepts do I want to develop?
The choice of software depends on how the school librarian
and/or teacher want to use it and what skills and concepts the pupils
should experience. There are, broadly, four skill categories: subject,
information handling, social and technical skills. Some programs are
subject specific i.e. concentrate on developing skills and concepts in
one subject area such as geography. For example, the PUDDLE
program[1] is used with pupils to examine the effects of water on the
land in terms of rainfall and landscape change. Other programs lend
themselves to the development of a combination of subject,
information handling and social skills – database, simulations and
modelling programs do this. All programs enable pupils to develop
technical skills by virtue of their using the technology.

Subject specific programs
Subject specific software deals with skills and concepts identified
with one part of the curriculum. This kind of software can act as a

visual aid or electronic blackboard and enables the teacher to present dynamic, colourful and complex images creating a more powerful and exciting lesson. The pupils can manipulate the data or screen image, experimenting and taking risks which can be swiftly deleted leaving a professional image on screen unspoiled by scratchings and rubbings out. An example of this type of program is DEWDROP[2] which allows pupils to examine how clouds are formed and different levels in temperature and height of clouds can be input by the teacher or pupils.

Database
Database programs are often described as empty shell, content-free and cross-curricular software. This type of program comes without any information in it. It is empty and therefore requires the user to input data. It is rather like an empty filing cabinet waiting for the files to go in. In creating these files or databases, pupils go through an information handling process, as was seen in Chapters 5 and 6. If the program is used in a field study in biology, for example the recording of all mini beasts in a defined grid square, a combination of information handling and subject skills are obviously developed at the same time. This also develops technical skills as the pupils learn to use the microcomputer while carrying out the project. Social skills too are fostered during the exercise. Pupils learn to work together, accept delegation of certain tasks and coordinate their work. An important element in this kind of work and one which is often overlooked, is the discussion which takes place. Cummings[3] suggests that the microcomputer is a powerful generator of discussion which should be fostered and not ignored and states that

> Language has a triple function in education: for communication, as a thinking tool and as a shaper of meanings. It is to be regretted that teachers dwell disproportionately on the first of these in conventional classroom for the sake of a permanent record. Talk is evanescent but writing leaves footprints.

Cummings further suggests[4] that certain aspects should be looked for in selecting software in order to encourage conversation and for pupils to see each other as resources:

1. a program with minimal screen output of words
2. relegation of the microcomputer to a passive role
3. withdrawal of the teacher from the discussion.

In order for these conditions to prevail it is essential that the pupils are able to use the software without the assistance of an adult. It must therefore be easy to load, run and manipulate.

With such conditions, Cummings continues, the observer would find pupils

    i)   completing their peers' unfinished sentences
    ii) encouraging others to contribute
    iii) inviting others to contribute
    iv) modifying another's statement
    v) offering evidence to support the foregoing.

In using viewdata software to create a database on FISHING with a group of boys in the school library (see Chapter 9, Figure 9.4), this author found the volume of discussion generated during their work to be surprising and exciting. Not only were the boys patient in explaining fishing techniques to their obviously ignorant librarian, but when they questioned each other's accuracy, they presented an argument and facts to support it in a calm and friendly manner. They were also able to accept criticism and questions without rancour and contributed to the analysis of their work, modifying it willingly.

2) What kind of learning process should the pupils experience?

According to Kemmis and Atkin,[5] there are four paradigms of software each creating a different learning experience. They are:

Instructional – drill and practice programs in which the microcomputer controls the learner through a series of questions which the pupil must answer before proceeding. This type of program is useful for remedial work, revision and reinforcement. If used constructively, instructional programs can be very effective but they can be very boring if they are used merely to transfer work to the microcomputer which would be better carried out in the traditional manner. Programs of this kind such as WORMS and DRAG are used to give pupils practice with addition or multiplication and often incorporate games into them. The major problem is that pupils may concentrate solely on the game aspect and also lose interest quickly.

Revelatory – simulations. This type of program creates a simulation of reality. The program mediates between the learner and the microcomputer allowing the pupil to learn by trial and error. Often a race against time, such programs can generate much excitement. A good simulation should be incorporated into a project and offer the opportunity to explore the subject from different angles, relate it to other subject areas and for extension work. Often this type of program requires a certain degree of pre-knowledge. The degree of pre-knowledge should be carefully assessed. Do the pupils have this? If not, how long and what is needed to bring them to the state of readiness and is it worth it? Is the topic relevant to the pupils and is the use of such a program the best means for pupils to experience this kind of topic? Should the programs be used in isolation or integrated into coursework? Simulation programs such as POND[6] which examines plant life in ponds and BRITISH ECONOMY[7] which allows pupils to examine variations in the economic health of the country are used across the curriculum and are often the best way to demonstrate an experiment in science or technology. It may be the quickest, cheapest and safest way of demonstrating a dynamic process in the class or laboratory. However, there is a danger that the real life experience may be replaced by the quick and easy screen image.

Conjectural – modelling programs. This category gives the pupils even greater control over the learning process by allowing them to input data and manipulate it in various ways. In this type of program, the pupils create a model of a situation and test it to see how it reflects reality. FISCAL,[8] an economics program creates a model for the management of the British economy.

Emancipatory – variously described as 'empty-shell' and content-free and as a labour-saving device and tool for learning. Database software falls into this category. Some database software comes with content for pupils to use as a source of information e.g. QUEST. Just as books come in a variety of formats so does computer software. Viewdata software such as COMMUNITEL, with pages downloaded from Prestel, comes closest to the description of a book with pages and page numbers. Spreadsheets, word processing packages and database management programs such as SIR or KWIRS can be seen as emancipatory programs. In this category, the pupil is in total control of the computer, inputting her/his own data and manipulating it according to need.

3) How should the class be organized?

When evaluating a program for selection, the school librarian and teacher should consider how the pupils are to be organized when the software will be used. This may be in the form of small groups, individual work, the whole class working together, and it may involve the use of multi-media resources or it may be a circus arrangement.

If small groups of say three pupils per microcomputer, then the teacher has to decide whether the program will run without her/his intervention. One particularly important point here is whether the programs are easily 'crashed', if for example, a pupil presses the

break key. The teacher should not have to constantly check each group to avoid such a situation. Easy to load and difficult to crash software is vital in a multi-work station class, as it releases the teacher to provide intellectual guidance rather than simply providing the services of a technician.

Small group work is ideal for investigative work using any of the four paradigms of software seen above. Conversation can be generated by pupils using drill and practice software as well as database programs, in that the pupils often use each other as a resource for learning, drawing upon each others' pre-knowledge and experience.

Individual work can be catered for by drill and practice programs and pupils who have advanced beyond others or who have a problem in class, may move aside to the microcomputer and go through a program which acts as a revision aid or reinforcement medium. This type of program can be used by the individual during lesson time or borrowed to be used in their own time in the school library.

Programs may also be suitable for use as part of a multi-media exercise. For example, pupils working on a project investigating living costs may use an on-line information system such as Prestel, viewdata to present their material and a spreadsheet package to present their costings. In this way, software can be integrated in the context of an assignment and no particular emphasis is put on any one medium. The focal point of the assignment is not the software, nor the medium, but the skills and processes which pupils go through within a particular context.

Obviously the software must be easy to use and manipulate, requiring the minimum of pre-knowledge and training. The best programs allow the teacher to gain basic skills in using them and to hand them over to pupils after a short introduction. The pupils learn by trial and error, by using the programs in context. In order to produce their results, they need to use the microcomputer and the equipment and the focus is therefore, not on the keyboard but on the screen. This author worked with one teacher who was plunged into a viewdata exercise with 12 pupils and four microcomputers but with no knowledge of the software. The pupils had none either. At the end of the project, the pupils were the experts and the teacher had advanced a little further. She had the skill, courage and creativity to facilitate the learning process of these pupils. She had created the situation in which the pupils had learned, had acted as mediator and had controlled their learning process. Software should offer the opportunity for the teacher and pupils to learn together. Whatever the nature of the program, the teacher and the pupils have the opportunity to investigate and discover together whether through discussion and argument, using drill and practice programs or through simulations, modelling or database programs.

4) Does the software fit into the curriculum?

In terms of examinations, school librarians and teachers have to be aware of examination requirements and ensure that the software chosen for part of any course fits into the examination requirements as laid down by examination boards.

The work done by pupils in using software programs will have to be assessed in some formal manner. Software of any kind needs to be carefully structured into the curriculum and not merely used as an interlude in the learning process to relieve boredom and offer variety, although it may do this as well. In this case there is every reason why the value accruing from the software should be recorded to the benefit of the pupils. Both teacher-initiated and pupil-initiated assessment questions should be formulated for the particular piece of work which incorporates the use of the program.

Programs chosen must also be relevant to the subject matter being studied by pupils and not artificially inserted into the curriculum. The software must relate directly to the way in which the subject is being taught in a particular school and one disadvantage of generally produced software, in history for example, is that it may be relevant in one school but not in another.

Time is a vital factor. Can the software be readily and easily integrated into the syllabus without undue stress? There should not be a need to reorganize the whole time-scale of a current course merely to fit the software into the work schedule. While this may be attractive to pupils, eager to use the microcomputer, it is an example of technology-led use of the software (see Chapter 7). The teacher has to decide whether the software will be central to the course or whether it will be a small part which will enhance and refine the course or work.

The teacher may also wish the software to offer the opportunity for extension work, to draw the subject being studied out further, relate it to other subject areas, raise issues and add a new dimension to the work e.g. the software on the economy allows pupils to learn skills of manipulating variables and such skills are cross-curricular. Often the same course can be duplicated, to advantage, using a microcomputer program. A written paper – a story or a report, can be used with the word processing software or viewdata software and be rewritten, providing another opportunity to refine and enhance the work in a new dimension.

Those selecting software in schools have to ask whether the software is likely to change or undermine the current curriculum. If it is used unimaginatively, the microcomputer can be nothing more than a child-minding device aimed to drill certain concepts and skills into pupils with the minimum of teacher intervention. Drill and practice programs can fall prey to bad practice and school librarians should question the acquisition of such software for use in the classroom or school library if it merely reinforces outdated teaching methods which are probably more effectively carried out using the blackboard and the verbal question and answer routine. Used as an additional resource, a different dimension which adds to an otherwise laborious process, programs can be very effective. Each type of program can act as a gateway to learning as well as a barrier in the process of learning. It is a question of identifying the best possible application as one of many partners in the learning process. The POND software, for example, displays complicated graphs on screen showing activity in the pond at different times of the year. It would take a teacher a great deal of time to prepare such graphs manually but more importantly the software allows pupils to manipulate it to discover aspects of pond life for themselves. It is also possible to relate the use of the software with field trips, work with other materials in the library and mathematical skills.

Secondary considerations
5) Practical problems – points to look out for

Documentation is vital to the ease of use of software of all kinds. Good documentation should be able to provide the potential user with a number of answers at a glance. The practising teacher or school librarian does not have time to go leisurely through pages of details which are poorly printed on A4 which are folded and tucked in an envelope with a disk. Users rightly expect the same standard of packaging as is found with other resources such as books and audiovisual material.

Good documentation will include tutorial and program guides, workcards, data sheets and other materials forming part of the scheme of work. Both the program and tutorial guides should be in booklet form. Large, clear headings should greet the eye with equally clear and brief paragraphs which can be quickly scanned. Diagrams and illustrations giving examples of screen output and prints-out also help users to get an idea of what the program is like.

The tutor's guides should contain program information i.e. the nature and content of the program. The target audience should be identified giving details of level and syllabuses to which the program relates. The amount of preparation which is required before the program can be used is important. Users need to know what peripherals are needed such as printers (and the makes of printer which can be used with the program) or robot arms or whether a joystick is needed. Information should also be given on how to connect the peripherals and operate them.

Details of different methods of using the program and examples of classroom practice will be helpful. Some documentation gives advice on how to use a program, for example as a visual aid, as a student resource or as part of a group activity. Suggestions for extension work should have been thought out by the publishers, also follow-up assignments and how the software might be fitted into further schemes of work or related to other subject areas. This is particularly important in relation to the GCSE examinations which require syllabuses to have a cross-curricular perspective, relating subjects to other subject areas and also to take into consideration the social, economic, environmental and other implications.

The second aspect of documentation to be considered is program notes. These should again be clear and concise. Program notes should inform the user what microcomputer the software is designed for, the disk track size e.g. 40 or 80 track, and whether a single or dual disk drive is required.

In terms of resources, the school librarian and teacher need to consider whether the software needs any additional resources before it can be used effectively. Will there be a need for workcards, data recording sheets, data disks, maps, atlases, pixel pads or coloured pens to accompany the software?

Maintenance of data is important in software in which data is created by pupils, for example in some mathematical or economics programs, in viewdata software or in databases. In some programs files have to be inverted overnight and this requires the microcomputer to be switched on over a long period of time. The sorting of data should also be simple and reasonably quick especially if pupils are using the program. Editing facilities in viewdata or database programs should be available and it should be possible to change records, delete data, move up and down the screen and save data.

Preparation time is a vital consideration in planning to use the software as well as in actually using it. Teachers and librarians need to know how long it will take for the teacher or librarian and pupils to learn how to use the program. The more complex software is the less usable software. Very good software allows the user to pick it up, scan the documentation, follow basic instructions and in under thirty minutes produce results. Good software could be said to provide two levels of usage – idiot and expert. Some database programs, for example, allow use at the most basic level and produce the required results. As the user becomes more experienced, her/his needs become more sophisticated and the user can go on to explore the more specialist facilities and techniques of the program and learn how to use it more expertly. FLEET STREET EDITOR, discussed in Chapter 3, is a good example here. A program which depends on several hours of training does not allow for the time and number constraints of the classroom.

A classroom or school library-based test is often the only method of ensuring the suitability of software. A development which allows classroom evaluation is the telesoftware service available from Prestel (see Chapter 7) which allows samples of programs to be downloaded and evaluated in school. The full program can be ordered after the school evaluation.

All programs need to be considered in terms of 'crashability' and those selecting software should try to discover in advance what facilities are in-built to protect users' data, if for example, the **break** key on the BBC-B microcomputer is pressed. The program should allow for this and should, at minimum take pupils back to a main menu or to the start of the program.

On-screen instructions should be clear and consistent. A simple, single line instruction or question, in straightforward language, will save endless searching of the documentation trying to work out what to do next. The term 'user-friendly' is often misused but related to software for use in schools, it should mean that pupils of different ability and reading levels should be able to understand instructions and where possible, **help** messages should be fitted into the program.

Design and layout of screen information is seen as expecially important in terms of pupils reading for information on the microcomputer. Many pupils have been found to take more care in reading information on a computer screen because they are more motivated in tasks involving the microcomputer. Software should not work against this by poor layout. The design should not be dull and colour should be used where possible and appropriate. Such factors are considered important when choosing books and audiovisual materials for the school library and are no less important in software selection.

6) Technical points

The documentation or disk sleeve should state whether the program is for network microcomputers, 40 or 80 track disk drives or cassette recorder. It should also state what memory capacity is required and, with database management programs, how many records can be saved on one disk. With some software the user is required to make backup copies of the master disk before use and the documentation should make it clear how this should be done.

Finding out about software
The first step in the process of selecting software is to find out what is available. This is a time-consuming task as the information on software is widely distributed between the printed and institutional sources. There is no single source and no national catalogue as there is for books. Tagg and Templeton[9] in their survey of the distribution of software, found that there is a serious communication gap between the producer and potential user. Although there is currently a software 'explosion', methods for the dissemination of information on software are numerous and varied.

Publishers
Mainstream sources of information about software are the large publishing houses, microcomputer manufacturers and software houses. Leading publishers disseminate information in two ways. The most common is to send out detailed descriptions of the software giving subject area, level, program details and a note where the program itself may be used. Secondly, they may send both the documentation and the program to the potential purchaser allowing a limited period during which the package can be used and evaluated. This may be on a sale or return agreement without asking for payment. Alternatively, customers are requested to pay first, with the offer of a refund if the program proves unsuitable. One problem for publishers is the ease with which much software can be copied and in some cases they are reluctant to send out a whole package.

Exhibitions
Another useful way of finding out what is available from publishers is to visit their stands at exhibitions. The best exhibitions are those which specialize in education. Most exhibitors have microcomputers on the stand and allow visitors to run the software there and then. This is a very useful way of gaining a first impression of a program and other teachers or school librarians may be present who have used the software in class and have evaluated its use. Following this pre-evaluation, it may be useful to ask for an inspection copy to be sent to the school for trial.

Education centres
Equally as important in keeping a regular check on publishers' output are those organizations which offer an advisory service for educational users. Software is held by these organizations and made available to potential users to evaluate. The Advisory Unit for Computer Based Education (AUCBE) in Hatfield and the Microelectronics Support Units with regional centres throughout the

country are examples. Local education authorities provide a similar service through educational computing centres, where they have been established. Although practice varies, users can visit such centres during regular weekly open evenings or during in-service courses which focus on specific programs and their curricular application. School library services are also now increasingly building up software collections, allowing school librarians and teachers to see demonstrations of software.

It is a good idea to establish a habit of visiting these centres regularly after school to look at software and discuss applications and practice with others. It is useful to plan a programme of visits, investigating software on one subject at a time. Visits can be made jointly by teachers and librarians. One drawback here is, because of copyright problems, most centres do not allow school staff to take software away and it cannot, therefore, be properly evaluated in the context with pupils in class or in the library.

Periodicals

The next level of sources are the computing magazines, journals and electronic newspaper reviews. These enable users to keep abreast of curriculum developments, styles of learning, classroom management, ideas for schemes of work and reviews of specific programs, often written by teachers who have tested the programs in a classroom situation. Popular magazines aimed at specific microcomputer users such as *Acorn User*, professional journals such as *Educational Computing* and the *Journal of Computer Aided Learning*, daily newspapers e.g. *Computer Guardian* and electronic sources such as Prestel, all provide good coverage of the subject.

Newsletters produced by computer user groups and societies also offer useful information on software. It is often not easy to find out what societies have newsletters or booklets available but an example is AYCE (Association of Young Computer Users) which is a subgroup of the British Computer Society.[10]

Catalogues

Last in the line of sources are the printed publications other than those listed above. Software catalogues and directories giving information on programs are largely available either by type of microcomputer, subject or type of educational institution. Most colleges of education libraries, for example, will have lists of software held in the college and organizations such as SMDP, (the Scottish Microelectronics Development Project), produce annotated catalogues of software available to schools at low cost. Catalogues and directories are often difficult to trace and it may be more worthwhile to find some reliable programs through known sources. If the program has potential, it is likely that the publisher is going to bring it to the school's notice or it will be mentioned in articles on computer applications in, for example, the *Times Educational Supplement*.

For school librarians, providing information on microcomputer software is now a normal part of their current awareness and selective dissemination of information service in schools. It is important for school librarians to scan computer journals, obtain information from publishers and other sources, arrange exhibitions of software in the school or provide loan copies of software from the school library service. The school librarian may be the person who controls the acquisition and borrowing of software and therefore has a responsibility to ensure that software which is borrowed is not copied in school, as this could lead to prosecution. Organizations such as FAST (Federation Against Software Theft) have been established to protect the copyright on software.

The selection of software for use in the school library or in the classroom should be a joint process involving the school librarian and teachers. As with the selection of other materials, the combination of the teacher's subject knowledge and awareness of subject curricular needs and the school librarian's bibliographic knowledge and awareness of cross-curricular resource needs should ensure that software which is purchased should be relevant to the pupils. Some schools have managed to have a policy laid down whereby all software which comes into the school, whether purchased by the library or by departments, is first catalogued and classified by the school librarian, thereby ensuring that a comprehensive catalogue (available on disk and print-out) can be maintained.

The following case study illustrates some of the points covered above in the selection of appropriate software.

Camden School for Girls
The librarian has been teaching information skills for many years and has found that local viewdata is an excellent coordinating device for a whole range of useful skills. Pupils become involved in the collection and manipulation of data and are motivated by the validity of the end product so that projects lose the contrived nature which marred many projects in the past. Identification of keywords and the sequencing of events lead easily into summary and use of skills such as skimming, scanning and highlighting. Presentation of findings is made more exciting and has the added bonus of a 'perfect' final copy which becomes a resource for others to use. The librarian

has also found that close examination of data required in producing databases brings about an awareness of bias and the development of objective criticism. The hierarchical structure of local viewdata has been found useful in the teaching of classification and in the sorting of ideas from the general to the specific which has proved helpful in note making, especially in the graphic form.

Acquisition of software

The objective was to acquire software which would stimulate interest in every subject. Because of the difficulty of assessing software before purchase i.e. the lack of objective reviews at the time and the fact that no 'on approval' facilities were available, several bad purchases were made when software was first acquired. The staff were very critical of much that was offered and a survey of their requirements revealed that:

1. Staff much preferred the 'empty shell' type of program which enabled them to put in their own subject content.
2. Staff wanted material which they could use with class groups.

It was decided that the school would provide packages for the following functions:

1. word processing for staff and pupils
2. database creation
3. local viewdata/teletext simulation

and that, in future, other software could only be purchased if it had been seen and appraised.

Promotion and use

Pupil use

There is tremendous enthusiasm for microcomputer use in school. The computing option for the fourth-year pupils was oversubscribed and the girls undertook fund raising in order to purchase more equipment so that larger numbers could be accommodated. The computers in the school library are available for use all day. One microcomputer is set up for word processing and can be used by pupils at any time, another is used as a Prestel terminal and the third is available for the use of a variety of CAL programs. The school librarian teaches information technology awareness to first-year pupils within the context of the library induction course, to third-year pupils as part of the integrated studies course (a proficiency certificate in basic computing skills is issued after this course), to fourth-year pupils within the social studies core and to sixth-form pupils in general studies sessions. The library opens at 8.15 am and from then until 9 am and from 3.45 pm to 4.30 pm, time is set aside for computer games as long as the microcomputers are not required for more serious work. Recently the microcomputers have been used for competitions during break-time to raise money for charity.

Librarian's use
The librarian sees information technology as another resource in the efficient provision of information. It is seen as very helpful in some areas but entirely unsuitable in others. Information technology can be used to coordinate traditional resources and make their use more effective and is of great value in teaching information and learning skills. An awareness of information technology and its implications for the future is seen as vital for the school librarian. The policy is to educate pupils to cope with the technology and give them the opportunity to exploit it in their future work and leisure.

In the school library, time constraints make it impossible to do everything the school librarian would like to do in microcomputer applications. Databases have been created using SIR to record a special collection of A-level background reading and a selection of fiction chosen by third-year pupils. A database relating to the school's archive collection is being compiled by sixth-form pupils during general studies sessions. The archive collection consists of some 500 items including photographs and documents. KWIRS is being used for this purpose. The library's subject index has been produced on a word processor and is now recorded on separate files for each letter of the alphabet. This means that any one section can be amended and reprinted easily.

The librarian has used COMMUNITEL local viewdata software as an electronic blackboard to coordinate the work of a group, a database of information to start a project, an electronic reading list and, by pupils, to present their findings in a professional way. The use of COMMUNITEL has involved much off-screen work and the 'empty shell' nature of the software leaves the subject content in the hands of the teachers. Pages have been downloaded from PRESTEL to provide additional material for teachers and pupils.

Software selection and use in this school has been guided by the policy stated above and it was not until such policy decisions were taken that appropriate software could be chosen.

References

1. See also Kelly, A. V. ed., *Microcomputers and the curriculum*, Harper & Row, 1984, 132.
2. See also Maddison, A., *Microcomputers in the classroom*, Hodder and Stoughton, 1982, 100.
3. Cummings, R., 'Small group discussion and the microcomputer', *Journal of CAL*, 1, (3), December 1985, 157.
4. *Ibid.*, 154.
5. Kemmis, S. *el al.*, *How do students learn. Working papers on CAL.* Occasional paper 5, C.A.R.E., University of East Anglia.
6. Maddison, *op. cit.*, 114.
7. Kelly, *op. cit.*, 132.
8. *Ibid.*, 133.
9. Tagg, W. and Templeton, R., *Computer software: supplying it and finding it*, British Library, 1983, 40.
10. The address for AYCE is MUSE, PO Box 43, Hull HU1 2HD.

Chapter 9
Microcomputers and in-service training
by Virginia A Berkeley and M W Paton

Introduction
In this chapter, two case studies are provided to demonstrate the need for careful planning by and for leadership from those responsible for the in-service training of school librarians and teachers.

Case study 1: Bedfordshire by Virginia A Berkeley
Although there will always be enthusiastic individuals who will teach themselves how to use a microcomputer, any concerted and coordinated attempt to develop effective use of the microcomputer in school libraries will depend heavily on an effective in-service training programme. A programme for in-service training provides the opportunities for focusing on certain priorities and policies, helps to ensure that the worst pitfalls are identified and (ideally) avoided and provides a framework within which development can be planned and expertise shared. In-service training takes up much time and expense, items in short supply in schools and school library services. Therefore there is a need to balance the demands of in-service training for effective development with restricted sources of time and money and this can cause difficulties. In Bedfordshire, these problems were tackled by adopting a 'cascade' approach to training. This is by no means a unique model, but it has proved an effective one and our experience of it is presented as a case study of a learning experience through which, as in all learning experiences, learning resulted from mistakes as well as from successes.

Initiating the use of microcomputers in school libraries
When the Department of Industry announced its 'Microcomputers in schools' scheme in 1980, it seemed to provide an opportunity for promoting the use of the microcomputer in school libraries and through that further to promote the school library. Initially, schools were only to have one microcomputer, so there was an argument for making the microcomputer available to the whole school by placing it in the school library. There was evidence that opportunities existed for linking the use of the microcomputer with information skills in work done on the SIR project, the availability of software such as QUEST and the potential of links with PRESTEL. These ideas were

116

discussed with the maths and computing adviser, who subsequently wrote to all schools suggesting that the microcomputer might be placed in the library and that it would be advisable for schools to have their school librarians attend in-service courses on microcomputer use which this adviser was organizing. This early collaboration with the adviser proved to be mutually beneficial as it was an attempt by the adviser to persuade schools to place microcomputers *away* from the maths or physics department and helped in the school library service policy of validating the links between the school library and information technology.

The training programme and cascade group

The first courses to be organized were two one-day courses for school librarians, the first being a 'hands-on' session to introduce everyone to the RML 380Z microcomputer, which was then the recommended machine. A follow-up course in 1982 on 'How to use the computer in the library' dealt with information handling software and how to use it (Figure 9.1). These courses were organized by the author and the maths and computing adviser, whose staff assisted on the courses.

Figure 9.1: Using new technology in school libraries, October 1982, programme

9.15	Assemble and introduction
9.30	COMPUTERIZED INFORMATION RETRIEVAL METHODS AND THE MICROCOMPUTER Heidi Ebrahim
10.15	Coffee
10.45	INFORMATION RETRIEVAL SYSTEMS AND THE SCHOOL LIBRARY Jean Beck
12.00	DEVELOPING A REGIONAL DATABASE Mike Blakey
12.45	Lunch
2.00	PRESTEL AND ITS IMPLICATIONS Jean Beck
3.15	Tea
3.30	HOW DO WE GET STARTED?

Questions and panel discussion. The panel, chaired by Virginia Berkeley, will consist of Jean Beck and John Warwick (General advisor for mathematics and computer-based education).

It was then decided that progress would be made if use was made of the 'cascade' method, in which a small group would receive intensive training and practice and would then train others. A computer pilot group (the cascade group) was formed of six librarians who had microcomputers in their libraries and the group began meeting in December 1982. Help was also given by the local MEP adviser.

The aims of this group were:

1) To provide a support group for the librarians and a channel for advice, information and policy from the author and outside advisers.

2) To encourage each member to develop particular expertise so that s/he would act as a focus for training others.

3) To provide a forum for discussing activities and avoiding mistakes such as attempting to create new programs when commercial packages were available. To encourage the use of the microcomputer for information skills development as opposed to traditional library housekeeping.

4) To develop a spread of expertise by asking group members to concentrate on particular uses of the microcomputer or on particular software packages. This aspect has developed with the increase in the availability of software. One advantage Bedfordshire has at this time was that packages such as SIR, EDFAX and COMMUNITEL were being piloted in the county and one librarian was involved in a Prestel project. This strategy helped individuals to develop confidence and expertise in their own chosen area without the pressure to become experts in all fields of microcomputer use.

5) The main priority was to develop databases which could be shared between members of the group and used as introductory material for school librarians who had newly acquired microcomputers.

The work of the cascade group
Between 1982 and 1984, the group increased from six to 19 participating librarians. In this period, the BBC microcomputer became the accepted machine, so much new learning had to take place. As well as discussing experiences and problems in handling microcomputers, the group looked at programs available and experimented with using them in a variety of ways.

The EDFAX software was used in Sandy Upper School to create an electronic school news bulletin. This was created by pupils and included a 'new books' item. EDFAX was also used in Stratton Upper School and Putteridge High School to create library guides, helping pupils to find resources and giving guidance on project work.

Database creation was a major theme in microcomputer use and Stratton Upper School had databases on fiction and on local history resources in the school, both using the QUEST software. MICROQUERY was used in Harlington Upper School to create a database on village history, using local census returns. Both the librarian and humanities teachers were involved in the use of the database, where pupils were encouraged to create as well as use files and it was found that much valuable discussion on both historical aspects and on the use of information was involved.

Some librarians also experimented with MASTERFILE to keep records of books and other materials on order. Within a year, enough work had been done to hold a training 'circus' (Figure 9.2) where the group demonstrated the information and expertise gained to other school librarians.

Figure 9.2: Microcomputer Update for School Librarians, September 1983, programme

The pilot group of librarians on micros in the school library have now been working for a year familiarizing themselves with programs and preparing sample databases. This is an opportunity for everyone to gain from their experience and to investigate how some of these programs might be used in each school.

PROGRAMME

9.15   Assemble and coffee
           divide into groups for:
   A.   MICROQUERY – the census database – Kathy Morris (Harlington Upper)
   B.   QUEST – an energy database – Chris Pipe (Lea Manor High)
   C.   SIR – an energy database – Hilary Boase (John Bunyan Upper)
   D.   CLAIRE – a local resources database – Mike Blakey (Computer unit)
   E.   EDFAX – a Ceefax simulation – Gill Grattidge (Stratton Upper)
   F.   Setting up a database – a case study – Isabella Coles (Denbigh High)

This is an opportunity to look closely at each programe, ask questions and try it out.

(All librarians attending spent 45 minutes with each package.)

All the above were valuable learning experiences for those involved, but were largely controlled by the school librarians, except for the Harlington project. It was then decided that more direct curricular involvement was necessary.

A TVEI project at Sharnbrook Upper school developed an IT course for TVEI pupils, using VUFILE software. The course was developed by the school librarian and some teachers. Pupils worked in both the school library and in the computer laboratory, learning both the technical skills of using information technology and information skills in the form of the creation of databases and discussion of the uses of files on different topics. For example, ATLAS was used as one topic and pupils created a file using six fields, including country, capital, currency and language.

At Icknield High School an ITAC (Information Technology Across the Curriculum) project was based on a previous project which had used EDFAX to create a library guide. Pupils were asked to extend this by creating information pages on reference books. Pupils worked cooperatively, both in the library and in the computer laboratory, under the supervision of both librarian and teachers, developing computer skills and communication skills. The pupils enjoyed the experience, as they were creating information which could be useful to other pupils. Figure 9.3 shows the school librarian's report on this project.

Figure 9.3: Report on the ITAC project at Icknield High School by Sheila Baker, Librarian
The aim of the project was to integrate the use of the computer with the teaching of library and information skills. Use will be made of the BBC-B microcomputer and the EDFAX software. A group of 26 pupils of both sexes were set the task of creating a database using a program which simulates teletext. Pupils were asked to create pages of information on a particular encyclopaedia or reference book. This information would then be saved on disk as part of the library information programme.

The class was divided into two groups, the first composed of more able and enthusiastic pupils while the second group was more reluctant. The pupils worked in pairs, investigating suitable books and filling in a checklist of information but with freedom to add additional information.

A brief demonstration of the program was given to pupils so that they could draw their layout on a screen planning sheet. Help was given here as they had limited experience of the program's limitations. Both the library and the computer room were used and pupils worked enthusiastically to create a range of pages, some with titles which were double-height, bi-coloured and flashed on and off.

The skills acquired include: cooperative working; researching, examining, selecting and rejecting information; systematic recording of information planning and presentation; and working within the limitations of the screen.

Comments
Pupils worked in pairs, choosing their own partners and all pairs were of the same sex. Most pairs shared the keyboard work scrupulously and while those with keyboard skills did not work much faster than the beginners, they were more adventurous in their layout. Pupils tended to use a variety of colours and they were keen to compare and criticize the results. All pupils enjoyed the exercise and were keen to do more. They gained satisfaction in producing information of direct use to others.

The COMMUNITEL software was piloted by the librarian at Houghton Regis Upper School. This package links the BBC microcomputer with Prestel and enables the user to download pages from Prestel and create databases using both locally produced pages and Prestel pages. Figure 9.4 is an outline of this project. A 'Fishing' database was created by four special needs pupils as well as community information files.[1]

Figure 9.4: Houghton Regis Upper School – Prestel in the curriculum
Aims
To use Prestel as a central school resource, located in the school library under the management of the librarian.

To involve colleagues in a team effort to use information technology to help pupils acquire information management skills. The librarian and the teacher work in partnership on course design and definition of objectives.

To utilize the special skills of the librarian – research and inquiry techniques and the teacher – experience, understanding and knowledge of the curriculum, to help pupils acquire skills which are applicable across the curriculum.

To devise a programme of in-service training for staff.

Learning objectives
To use viewdata to help pupils acquire information management skills.

To use viewdata software as a means of assisting pupils to work through the steps necessary in preparing and producing a project in a disciplined way.

To use viewdata to help pupils think about the structure and presentation of information and the limitations imposed by the format.

To use viewdata to help pupils acquire the techniques of revising, reviewing and editing their work.

To provide an opportunity for pupils to work cooperatively on devising and implementing a project.

To enable pupils to produce work on the computer which can be used by others, thus validating their work.

To provide an opportunity for pupils to experience new technology.

Use of Prestel and Viewdata
As a source of information.

As a medium for pupils to learn.

As a means of communication.

As an example of information technology available to business and industry.

As a source of computer software.

Benefits

Concepts	–	relevance, accuracy, bias, currency, suitability, value, need.
Attitudes	–	appreciation of need, heightening of critical awareness.
Values	–	cooperation, responsibility, self-evaluation, autonomy.
Experiences	–	meeting people, national and international awareness, community involvement, working on their own.
Skills	–	Information management: Analysis, design, planning, organizing and structuring information. Researching, selecting, rejecting, sorting.

Negotiations, interviews.
Interpreting, analysing, synthesizing, summarizing.
Evaluation, criticizing, editing.
Design: Screen design and layout.
Technical: Using microcomputers.

Copyright: Judith Askey 1985.

The important factors about these projects were that they were examples of *cooperative* projects linking the school library directly with the curriculum via the use of the microcomputer. In each case pupils were involved in database creation. By actively encouraging pupils to create information in databases, it was found that pupils were introduced to fundamental concepts of computerized information retrieval. It was discovered that emphasis should be placed on the *process* which pupils go through in handling information, rather than just the end product. The process is the essential feature in preparing pupils to cope with technological approaches to information retrieval systems, because it makes concrete to them many of the abstract concepts involved in understanding the nature and organization of information.

Training continues via sessions where current work in different areas is demonstrated to small circulating groups. New programs which are tested in schools are also shown on these training days. Important new developments, like Prestel Education Service are introduced to all school librarians (Figure 9.5). In this way, a general training model is followed by a cascade model, for example in the use of PRESTEL.

Figure 9.5: Prestel and Viewdata Course for School Librarians, April 1984, programme

10.30   Introducing PRESTEL and Viewdata
       Hilary Farnsworth MEP, CAIS Coordinator (Chiltern Region)
11.30   Hands on exercise using local viewdata packages
 1.00   Lunch
 2.00   Continuing hands on
 2.30   Integrating this resource into the curriculum
       Judith Askey, Houghton Regis Upper School
 3.00   Tea
 3.30   Managing and updating a school news database
       Chris Pipe, Lea Manor High School
       PRESTEL education service – CET project on IT
       Jo Taylor, CET

Training cannot solve all problems
Although the cascade approach has undoubtedly been effective, some mistakes were made and problems were identified. Expertise in certain areas was initially bound up in one person and therefore was lost when they left. This is improving but there will always be some enthusiasts who move ahead of the rest. The pattern is correct but more than one 'expert' on each package is clearly needed.

When the authority decided to move over to BBC microcomputers, there was a need to learn how to handle the new machines and the new software. Similar problems have arisen in schools which are using networks, as some of the existing software will not operate on the networks. A further problem can be when librarians and teachers learn how to handle and use particular software packages and are reluctant to try out newer packages which may provide easier and more effective ways of doing the tasks needed. Cascade training helps here to break down resistance to change. There was also the problem of getting schools to use the technology in the most effective ways and not merely creating technological versions of existing manual systems e.g. card catalogues. Only after they had used the microcomputer in this way, could school librarians move on to think in new ways about using information technology effectively.

Conclusions
In-service training on the use of microcomputers in schools requires commitment, hard work and an ability to be constantly learning in a new and fast-changing field. It can produce results – in closer involvement of school librarians in the curriculum, and improving the status of school librarians as well as the teachers' perceptions of the school librarian's role. The combination of the impact of information technology and the move towards more information-conscious independent learning strategies, embodied in the new curriculum initiatives such as TVEI, CPVE and the GCSE, ensure that the IT competent librarian has an important role to play in the school which is recognized and appreciated where it is offered.

Effective and well-supported in-service training for school librarians in information technology ensures that librarians have the confidence and the competence to undertake this curricular role. Bedfordshire's experience of the cascade model of training suggests that it provides a cost-effective method of providing training in both breadth and depth. It provides an avenue for using expertise effectively and readers will have noticed that the expertise was drawn from a wide range of sources, including national experts, local MEP centres, experts within the education service as well as the cascade group experts. This cooperative effort has helped librarians to cope with a huge and rapidly changing field, so that they are motivated to be involved. The results in terms of greater recognition of school librarians' expertise and closer involvement in the curriculum is already evident in many schools and it seems probable that information technology will provide school librarians with the most effective avenue yet available into the heart of the curriculum.

References
1. See for example Askey, J., 'An information frame-up,' *Times Educational Supplement*, 26/4/85, 9 and Askey, J., 'This isn't work, it's fun', *Educational Computing*, July/August 1985, 14–15.

Case study 2: Grampian Region by M W Paton

Background
Grampian Region has 40 secondary schools, all of them comprehensive. Of these, 15 are in the city of Aberdeen and the others are scattered throughout some 3000 square miles of north east Scotland. The furthest is 77 miles from Aberdeen where the central Schools Library Service (SLS) is situated.

All schools have some form of library staffing and at present half have full-time professional librarians, while the others are staffed by full- or part-time library assistants. A recent policy decision by the Education Department will ensure that within a few years, every school will have a professional librarian.

These two factors, distance and staffing, have a radical influence on the patterns of in-service training. For example, sessions involving all library staff are held in Aberdeen and to be viable are timed to run from 10 am to 4 pm. By contrast, training and development sessions are taken with smaller groups and at convenient centres throughout the region.

In-service on IT has been essentially empirical. Sessions have been organized as need was recognized and opportunity allowed. Throughout the programme, two objectives have been constant and can be simply expressed as

a) to demonstrate to all librarians the scope and potential of IT for their schools and,

b) to encourage and support the adoption and development of IT.

From a very early stage, the librarians separated themselves into two groups, those who were comfortable with IT and prepared to become involved, and those who were not. Before long those in the first group divided yet again into some who were enthusiastic and innovative and others who were less venturesome but prepared to operate at established routine levels.

The emergence of these groups presents both problems and opportunities. The main problem is that sessions which are intelligible and interesting to one group can be incomprehensible to others. The main compensation is that the small group of enthusiasts help to provide speakers, demonstrators and tutors for those in other groups.

Patterns of in-service training

Taking account of these broad influences, a pattern of in-service training has begun to emerge in Grampian. The following is an account of both successes and failures and of plans for the future. It attempts to demonstrate what can be learned from experience in meeting the needs of school librarians and to give some guidelines on how a programme of in-service training might be planned and implemented.

The first session involves all school librarians. Its objective is to approach the subject on a broad front, look at its potential, take account of difficulties, touch upon what is being done in some schools and indicate how a start might be made. Jargon is used minimally and one or at most two simple applications are demonstrated. These can involve running a careers program and demonstrating simple information retrieval techniques.

This is an appetite-whetting and confidence-building session. The speaker should be a librarian who is sympathetic to the problems of beginners. At the end, the librarians are invited to bring their doubts and problems individually to the SLS and they depart with an information sheet describing in non-technical language the value and potential of a library based microcomputer. These include

1. A microcomputer in the library is available for use by the whole school and the librarian can assist pupils to make use of it.

2. Programs can be centrally held and used in the library as well as in departments.

3. Text files on subjects studied in depth can be prepared to suit teachers' needs.

4. The librarian can help to incorporate computerized methods into the school's information skills programme.

5. Personal reading can be supported by fiction text files, lists of

additions to stock and pupils' book reviews.

6. Linked with viewdata, access is given to external databases: sections can be downloaded and thereafter processed free of charge.

The next step is to provide training sessions in the form of workshops, held at various central points throughout the region. They will involve small groups with a microcomputer for at most every two trainees and a practised librarian to help at each microcomputer. They open with a short explanatory introduction and go over as soon as possible to 'hands-on' experience. The programs used need to be unsophisticated at this stage. Most of the time is spent on the microcomputers but the group is called together for a final session and discussion.

Information sheets which give detailed, practical information, and assume no prior knowledge can be distributed. The content and level of presentation of these sheets might include:

Do make a case for your own library-based microcomputer; borrow a machine if you cannot have your own; speak to interested teachers about support for their subject.

Don't attempt to computerize the full catalogue; don't try to use the microcomputer initially for an issue system; don't worry about learning to program – it isn't necessary.

Opportunities e.g. free software, advice and support which is available; and opportunities for real cooperation with teachers.

How to make a start: at one of these levels
 a) Without a microcomputer – make a case based on the 'Potential uses' document.
 b) With a microcomputer – for work with a datafile, find an interested teacher, talk over the information support the microcomputer can provide, discuss the parameters of a project and the terms used by the teacher, and then create a small sample file showing how the subject spread and development of the project can be reflected by the datafile and the use of keywords.

Reading list – a short, realistic list, including the manual for the microcomputer in use, indicating the essential chapters in the manual and those which are not required for familiarization purposes.

Joint teacher/school librarian meetings
Although the presence of teachers may inhibit some school

librarians, a joint session may go a long way towards securing the commitment of a senior teacher who may in turn give valuable support to the case for library-based IT and encourage other teachers to make use of it.

Joint sessions can involve six to eight schools at a time. They deal broadly with the potential impact of IT on the school library as outlined in the 'Potential uses' list. More detailed attention is given to computerized information handling and its implications for teachers and pupils in terms of its educational value, its information value and the necessary computing skills. Retrieval based on keywords, the relationship of the keywords to the curriculum, various search strategies, the in-service needs of teachers, and the training required by pupils, are the subjects of immediate interest to teachers. Again relevant information sheets are circulated. A report on the meeting should be prepared and sent out to schools supplementing and reinforcing the verbal reporting of the teacher and the school librarian.

Induction courses
Newly appointed school librarians need an introduction to IT as it is practised in the region's school libraries. They need to know about the availability of hardware and software within their school, through the SLS and other sources, and they need practical training and advice on making a start or on achieving progress. Such courses also give SLS staff an indication of the school librarians who will need further individual training.

Practising librarians
School librarians who are using IT and have it effectively integrated into their ongoing services still have in-service needs. They are interested in developments undertaken by their colleagues and in others' experiences of the attitudes, responses and training needs of teachers and pupils. They welcome opportunities to discuss their successes and problems and to consider how further progress may be made e.g. trying out viewdata packages. They will want to know about developments both within and outside the region. They value the opportunity to meet other experts, in the field of education and computing and to have talks and demonstrations on technological and other advances.

Practising school librarians also have much to contribute to in-service training. They can be invaluable as speakers at lower-level sessions and in some cases can call at nearby schools to give information and advice, always taking into account the sensibilities of the school librarian receiving the visit.

Plenary sessions

There remains a need to introduce IT slots into general in-service sessions despite, or perhaps because of, divergences in skills, attitudes and achievements. The purpose of such sessions will be to remind everyone of continuing needs and opportunities and to foster an 'all in it together' spirit. The presentation takes account of different levels of comprehension and competence: ideally a fine balance is struck between bringing some pressure to bear on the reluctant, yet not increasing the worries of the faint-hearted. All this needs to be done in language free from computerese.

Home and invited speakers (see Figure 9.6) are suitable, providing invited speakers are well briefed in advance about their audience. The home team can deal with matters such as the authority's policy, hardware and software availability, support from SLS (e.g. a datafile exchange system), general levels of practice and examples of good practice in schools. Visiting speakers will be librarians and educationists rather than computer experts and can deal helpfully with such topics as the relevance of IT to the curriculum in general and to information skills in particular.

Figure 9.6: Microcomputers in the School Library course
A course for school librarians who already have some experience of using a microcomputer for information retrieval

9.30	Chairman's remarks R. Blackburn
9.45	Pupil-created datafiles Sandra Davison, Milne's High School
10.30	Coffee
11.00	The Disabled Project database Lynda Bain, Dyce Academy
11.45	Computerisation of AV and newspaper cuttings Ian Leith, Lossiemouth High School
12.30	Lunch
1.30	Microcomputers and fiction Iona Scott, Mintlaw Academy
2.15	The Microcomputer in the School Library Project Dorothy Williams, RGIT, SLIS.
3.00	Remote databases Lorna Stephen, Computer Department
3.30	What next? – open session

Specialist sessions

In-service meetings dealing with curriculum changes, information skills, and individualized learning provide opportunities to consider IT in a practical educational context and to explore its value in various applications.

Potential pitfalls

While most of the in-service training undertaken has been successful, some failures have also been experienced and the following observations should be useful to those planning in-service training.

Long sessions can be counterproductive. Using microcomputers is intellectually and emotionally demanding and a whole day's in-service entirely devoted to it may not achieve the objectives set.

External speakers are perhaps the greatest risk especially when they are not familiar with school libraries. In particular, enthusiasts are to be treated with caution. They are not noted for the perspective they bring to the subject, or for their understanding of the problems of beginners. Invited speakers should be carefully briefed on the topic they should deal with, the purpose of their contribution and the present achievements and problems of their audience.

The fears and worries of many school librarians are both real and complex. They range from a general tendency to go into shock when confronted with anything technological, to more particular fears of damaging the equipment or destroying the software. Using microcomputers can create very particular tensions especially in beginners and those affected need much patience and understanding.

It is usually more profitable to use school and SLS staff as far as possible as speakers and demonstrators. They will be known to their colleagues, their background is the same, they will be familiar with early difficulties and have succeeded in overcoming them. That colleagues of similar status are seen to have travelled the road successfully gives reassurance to others and lends credibility to each exercise. Furthermore, the experienced school librarians will enjoy outlining their achievements and being allowed to do so is a richly deserved encouragement.

Although the home team are generally the safest and most successful speakers, carefully selected visitors are necessary to deal with particular applications and developments and to contribute fresh ideas.

Coping under pressure

IT is a new area of involvement, additional to all other aspects of school librarianship. This creates problems for librarians in their schools – problems which must be acknowledged fully in in-service training. It also creates problems for SLS staff. Without additional staffing, it is impossible fully to encourage and support the adoption of and training in a whole new and highly specialized area of activity.

A related factor is pre-Associateship training which adds to the training load of SLS staff. Over and above the general in-service programme it is worthwhile holding an *ad hoc* IT session for pre-Associateship trainees. Differences in library school influence apart, those attending are likely to be at the same stage of awareness and level of motivation. Such sessions can concentrate on policy and practice within the authority and in addition to their immediate value, they help to show which trainees are likely to require particular support. Any such sessions can form part of the authority's pre-Associateship training programme and are doubly valuable.

To help SLS staff cope with the additional work involved, certain courses of action are open, although none are guaranteed success. Firstly, the parent body should be made aware of the additional burden and obligations. Alleviatory suggestions can be made and sympathetic senior staff may put forward ideas of their own and make additional resources available. Certainly, there is a strong case for this even where resources are scarce.

Secondly, the authority's training officer can be approached for support. The training department is often keen to know of situations in which they can become involved and they may offer administrative support and take on some of the organizational and clerical work involved.

Thirdly, the appointment of a training officer to the education or library department on a full-time basis may be proposed. Alternatively, training responsibilities may be added to other needs to enhance the case for an additional member of staff.

Finally, IT is such an important area of development as to present a strong case for the appointment of an IT officer to encourage and support its adoption throughout all schools. One of the duties of an IT officer would be in-service of all library and teaching staff at all levels. An IT officer has recently been appointed within the SLS.

Future developments
The cost of hardware is decreasing as fast as its efficiency is increasing. We can, therefore, confidently expect that the home computer now being used in schools, e.g. BBC, Apple and Spectrum will soon be replaced by more powerful personal computers like the IBM and Apricot. Enhanced with a hard disk and equipped with a suitable database management package like dBASE2, KMAN or SUPERFILE or better still, one of the new integrated IR and library

management packages like MICROLIBRARY or CALM, the new microcomputers will be capable of holding and processing the whole catalogue of a school library.

The implications of full-library or full-school automation are not irrelevant to our immediate needs and are worth anticipating at this stage. Clearly the in-service training will cover both user groups, the teachers and the librarians.

For school librarians, the necessary computing skills are unlikely to cause problems, especially where they have already been operating at home computer level. The principles on which larger packages operate are very similar to those retrieval programs for home computers. There are, however, substantial differences in the indexing and vocabulary control. Selecting keywords for a single subject file of some 200 entries is much more simple than selecting and controlling a vocabulary for a general database of 10–20,000 entries. Existing professional literature and educational thesauri tend to be of limited value. School librarians will need much help here, even allowing that it will be possible to download, edit and re-use entries created previously by colleagues.

Teachers will require advice on the value of automated retrieval and assistance in coping with its intricacies, along the lines described under 'Joint teacher and school librarian meetings'. The necessary in-service training will of necessity fall to the school librarian.

The school librarian's and teacher's role in teaching information skills to pupils is likely to be further enhanced by automation. As the roles of teachers and librarians become closer, both will need advice and in-service help from educationists on the curriculum and teaching/learning needs.

Conclusion

Information technology in general, and the applications of microcomputers in particular can be considered one of the most important developments in modern education. The technology is complex and subject to rapid change. Both school librarians and teachers will disregard it at their peril. The successful adoption of IT will depend in large measure on the quality of support including in-service training which those in schools are offered. A full, relevant and practical programme is therefore imperative.

Chapter 10
The future
by James E Herring

This chapter will attempt to provide school librarians and teachers with a brief outline of the future potential of information technology in tomorrow's schools. While predicting the future is a hazardous operation and while it not possible to put accurate figures on developments e.g. to say that in 10 years time every secondary school pupil will have a computer of some kind as part of her/his 'desk', some trends may be identified which may be helpful to those in education who wish to continue to develop the use of microcomputers in schools for educational purposes. The areas to be covered in this chapter will be future trends in teaching methods, developments in hardware and software, school information systems, external sources of information, expert systems, video and optical disks and the future role of the school librarian.

Teaching methods
There has been much stress in education recently on pupil-centred as opposed to teacher-centred education and this implies that teaching methods are likely to continue to move away from the traditional 'chalk and talk' methods (although these may still be appropriate to introduce pupils to a topic) where the teacher dominated the progress of each lesson and pupils remained fairly passive. More and more schools are examining whole-school policies on resource-based learning, incorporating an emphasis on information skills across the curriculum. This laudable trend could still take place without a single microcomputer being available in the school and thus the question must be asked – what salutary effects are developments in microcomputer technology and use likely to have on future trends in teaching methods? Kelly[1] states that the microcomputer, '. . . in presenting teachers with opportunities to extend the scope of their practice, faces them also with some important questions about what they are doing and why they are doing it'. It is only after such questions have been answered, Kelly argues, that the *future* potential of microcomputers can be realized. The need for all educators in schools, including school librarians, teachers and advisers must be to extend the possibilities of individual learning by using microcomputers to allow pupils to carry out activities in class and in

the library which were not possible before the computer revolution. The ability of microcomputers to produce simulations of real life, for example, should allow pupils greater opportunity and flexibility to recreate the outside world in the classroom and learn skills and concepts more easily.

Future teaching methods will obviously depend on the numbers of microcomputers available in schools and on teacher-training so that teachers are not hidebound by fears of lack of control over pupils working in a computer room. The trends of allowing individuals to work at their own pace, to experiment and to interact with computer programs which can be easily manipulated by teachers with few programming skills will continue. In school libraries, the emphasis on information skills, including information technology skills will be even more important as pupils have access to a wide variety of internal and external sources of information. A major part of the school librarian's and teacher's role will be educating pupils in the selection of relevant information from a bewildering variety of sources. The *rejection* of information by pupils is likely to be much more important than at present and teaching methods will have to take account of this.

One further change in teaching methods which information technology may allow is to give pupils much greater opportunity to teach themselves and to choose a variety of 'teaching methods' from the microcomputer. It is not inconceivable to visualize the existence of microcomputer programs which offer pupils a choice, in learning the concept of GRAVITY, for example, of learning by drill and practice, or by experimentation or simulation or modelling. The crucial question here will be whether the pupil will have the ability and experience to choose different methods but the increasing sophistication of computer programs should allow for in-built assessment of pupils using such programs, so that a pupil choosing an inappropriate method of learning would be directed to another method by the microcomputer. This does not mean teacher-free or librarian-free instruction. The teacher or librarian as intermediary will certainly become more common in the future. What will still remain, however, is that the teacher and school librarian will still control the aims and objectives of the learning process and the content. The microcomputer will merely allow greater freedom of choice.

Developments in hardware and software

In a recent television programme, *Microlive* on BBC1, it was suggested that in ten years time, microcomputers will be available which will fit into a present attaché case. These microcomputers will have built-in disk drives, a range of ROM chips to provide database management, word processing, spreadsheet and calculation facilities and will have, as standard 20 megabyte memories i.e. 40 times more memory than a standard school microcomputer at present. The possibilities of using such powerful microcomputers in schools will allow pupils, for example, to have disks containing a wide range of software for different curricular purposes. The same disk could then be used in different classes taken by the pupil.

For school librarians, the most immediate change is the introduction of hard-disk facilities for the present range of 8-bit microcomputers and for newer 16- and 32-bit machines. At present, Grampian Region School Library Service are engaged in a project using IBM microcomputers with hard disks to computerize the holdings of the school library service and the complete library stocks of two secondary schools.

This trend is inevitable and presents school librarians and teachers with opportunities and problems. The opportunities lie in the existence of OPACs (on-line, public access catalogues) which can be used by pupils to locate any sources of information in the school library or, indeed, anywhere in the school. This should not necessarily mean that subject-specific databases e.g. a database on GRAVITY for first-year pupils, will disappear. In fact, they will be needed to allow for distinctions in the use of materials by different levels of pupils. For example, sixth formers studying aspects of GRAVITY are likely to use a much more sophisticated language than first years and two different databases, using alternative keywords, may be needed. The problems inherent in OPACs lie in the indexing of materials and the vast amount of information available. To continue the above example, if a first-year pupil enters the keyword GRAVITY in the school's hard-disk microcomputer using a sophisticated database management program, s/he will be given a wide range of sources of information, books, periodicals, computer software, multimedia kits and videocassettes. Much of this information will not be suitable for this pupil and the school librarian's problems will lie in indexing materials to allow for access at different levels of ability but more importantly to ensure that pupils, through information skills teaching, are aware that they will have to use the OPAC in a different way from subject-based databases. At the same time, school librarians will not wish to restrict brighter pupils from using sources which might not be appropriate for their peers, thus the labelling of resources for S1/S2 or S6 may be counterproductive in hindering the independence of pupils in using resources.

Developments in software will include greater use of expert

systems (see below) but also a wider range of more sophisticated programs, including many more computer graphics than at present. Drill and practice programs will be available for pupils to use in school and at home (where sophisticated microcomputers will be commonplace) but greater emphasis will be laid on the in-house development of simulation and modelling software which are more pupil-controlled than at present.

A significant future development is likely to be the production of software which will run on different types of microcomputer. This is a major problem at present. Future microcomputers will have in-built cards which will be able to alter programs. Chambers and Sprecher[2] state that, 'Software advances can be expected to improve this automatic conversion problem, especially for the most popular microcomputers'. This will give schools two advantages in that they will not be restricted to buying software for one particular type of microcomputer and, also, they will be able to take advantage of newer microcomputers without fear of software incompatibility.

A further trend will be the increasing ability of microcomputers to be voice-activated i.e. to understand human speech and react to spoken commands from the user. One particular area commonly cited is the voice-to-print facility allowing the user to talk to the computer and have this speech printed out. An in-built word processing facility would enable the microcomputer to set out the document – report or essay – according to the user's choice. In the school library, databases may become voice activated and keywords or phrases may be 'said' to the microcomputer which will understand. There are obvious advantages here but voice-activated computers may have little more than technical advantages in education as it is the *content* of speech, not the fact of speech itself which is vital. As long as pupils learn how to think clearly about what they are going to 'say' to the microcomputer and realize any limitations which voice-activation may involve, this kind of development may be useful. For pupils with handicaps, voice-activation may be crucial in that it may allow them greater access to software, but the information skills of these pupils will still be paramount to the quality of their learning.

School information systems

At present in schools, microcomputers can be seen in small networks in 'computer rooms', individual microcomputers used in classrooms and school libraries may have one or more microcomputers available for a range of purposes. The likely trend in schools is for the whole school to be seen as a total information system in which all parts are interconnected, perhaps to a central supercomputer (a microcomputer capable of acting as a mainframe) containing large databases which can be accessed from any part of the school.

There are exciting possibilities here for school librarians, teachers and pupils. In school library terms, it will mean that the school library's information subsystem will be open to access from any part of the school. This means that a teacher or pupil wishing to check on a particular piece of information – the meaning of a word, the properties of a metal or the location of a place – should be able to access the school library's microcomputer(s), choose a particular database from a menu e.g. dictionary, check on the meaning of the word and obtain a print-out back in the classroom. Thus external use of the library is likely to grow rapidly but it should not be seen as a threat to the existence of the school library or information centre as it may be called. It is *use* of the school library's resources, whether internal or external that is important and the quality of information service is obviously improved if the end-user, whether teacher or pupil, is given instant access to information without the need to walk from one part of the school to another.

For school librarians, the existence of school information systems will allow a greater investigation of the information needs of teachers and pupils in the school. It is the school librarian who will have, via her/his education and training in information science, the knowledge to examine information needs and provide the relevant access to required information. Thus teachers planning new courses should be able to access the library's database to discover what resources exist in the school and outside the school in relation to a particular course. Information on new materials – catalogues, bibliographies, materiographies, software reviews, abstracts and indexes and full-text articles – should be available on-screen from any part of the school. An important aspect of information systems in organizations such as schools is the maintenance not of the hardware systems, which involve technical skills, but of the information held within the system. It is to the school librarian (or information manager) that future school administrators are likely to turn for advice on control of access to and organization of the vast amounts of information available in the school's information system.

For teachers, school information systems will allow pupils to work in one part of the school, possibly without supervision, while the teacher will be available for consultation through an electronic mail system, which will be an integral part of the total information system. Teachers will be able to advise pupils who need help with software or who wish to arrange a tutorial with the teacher. Again, such systems have to be seen not as threats to teacher control or pupil discipline but as providing advantages to teachers and giving them a role which caters more for the individual pupil than for groups.

Pupils use of the school's information system will obviously be limited. They will not, for example, have access to the school's administrative files but they will be able to download software from the school library database into classroom microcomputers and thus 'borrow' a resource from the library. They will be able to use the electronic mail system to leave messages with the school librarian in the form of reservations for books or audiovisual materials or requests for help in the location of information on topics not covered in the school library database. Pupils will be able to use electronic mail to communicate with each other and to discuss curricular work as well as sending personal messages. The fears of teachers and librarians that electronic mail systems will merely become electronic CBs (Citizen Band Radios) will be overcome when pupils are taught the value of communicating with each other during coursework. Finally, pupils will have access, through the information system to large-scale computer memory which will allow them to use sophisticated word processing packages to produce projects and essays of a high standard of presentation, incorporating text and graphics.

External sources of information

As was seen in Chapter 7, schools now have access to a wide variety of external sources of information via Prestel and databases accessed via Prestel. This is an area which is likely to expand rapidly in the near future.

Schools will be involved in networks on a local and national basis, with schools in different parts of the country being able to access information being held in other schools. This will provide the opportunity to share in software and coursework design as well as facilitating inter-library loans between schools. Local networks may be able to provide school librarians with access to computerized databases of the local public, college or university library, thus giving pupils potential access to all the library resources in one particular area. The complete holdings of all school libraries in one region may be held in a central database organized by the school library service and this may allow schools to share in the acquisition of costly materials, thereby saving money.

The growth in external databases providing information will also grow rapidly. The School Curriculum Development Committee recently published a directory of computerized information sources in education and is encouraging the creation of educational databases. Future databases will provide information for teachers and librarians to use in the selection of materials. For example, a biology teacher preparing a course on the human body will be able to access databases which will provide examples of such curricula in other schools, the teaching methods used and the resources used. Other databases will provide not only bibliographic details of educational resources such as books, slide-sets and software but will provide annotated evaluation by teachers who have piloted software or used printed sources in the class.

Electronic publishing is also likely to revolutionize access to external sources of information. As more periodicals in particular become available only in an electronic form, schools will have unlimited (except by economic constraints) access to full-text educational information. Thus a teacher, pupil or school librarian seeking information on a particular topic will be able firstly to use an electronic abstracting service which will give details of what is available in periodical literature and then follow up this by accessing periodicals on-line. By paying a certain sum for each article accessed and possibly downloaded on to disk in the school library, the user will not only be able to read the article, but to keep it for further use. Copyright problems are inevitable in this area but it is certain that in a few years time electronic publishing of periodicals will be the norm rather than the exception.

For school librarians and teachers, this means that the school library, through which these external databases may be accessed, will become not just a localized store of information but an information link to a multitude of other sources of information. Again, the needs of the curriculum will determine which databases are used and there will be a limited amount of money available for such access. It will therefore require policy decisions by librarians and teachers on what proportion of the budget of the school library or school departments should be spent on accessing external sources. It is also, of course, inevitable that schools with better financial resources or with more access to external sources of finance, such as PTAs, will provide pupils with the opportunity of using a greater variety of external sources of information. .

In the future, the school library itself may well be seen as an external source of information by pupils. It has been argued that future schools will provide only part-time education for pupils as many pupils will spend most of their 'educational' day working on a home computer which has access to the school via a telephone line. The pupil will simply download a piece of coursework which may involve drill and practice programs or simulation work but may also require the pupil to access sources of information from the school library or information centre. A pupil studying ANIMAL BEHAVIOUR, for example, may work with a simulation of birds learning to fly and may have to write an assignment, using a word processor on how birds communicate. The pupil could then access the library database by keyword or by inputting certain questions to the database, and be put on to a full-text database giving information on this topic. Importantly, despite the advances in technology and the *access* to information, the educational end-product will still be evaluated on the pupil's *use* of the information and a demonstration of whether s/he has learned concepts and skills.

Expert systems

Stonier and Conlin define expert systems as, '. . . intelligent databases which do not merely regurgitate information but which can actually provide professional advice'.[3] The potential use of expert systems in education may provide an opportunity for teachers and school librarians to provide pupils with reliable sources of information which can be asked questions in natural language and can be programmed and provided with data to answer questions input by pupils. An expert system is tied to a particular *domain* of knowledge. For example, expert systems are now common in medical diagnosis, in which a doctor can input symptoms of a patient and be given a probable diagnosis and expert systems have been found to improve, but not act as a substitute for, the diagnostic skills of doctors. Thus in future schools, there may be expert systems in particular subject areas but these will be narrow areas. It is unlikely that an expert system in GEOGRAPHY will be possible, because of the sheer amount of 'expert' information needed to form the *knowledge base* upon which the system works. It will be possible to have expert systems on for example, agricultural systems. The pupil will be able to use the expert system to learn about a particular topic by asking certain questions of the computer and being provided with answers in a variety of forms. The system may provide the pupil with definitions; may give the pupil an exercise to complete and the pupil may key in information or talk to the computer; may provide a link to a videocassette or disk (see below); or may connect the pupil to an existing database in the school.

The major problems in relation to expert systems is their reliability – the medical systems are not foolproof and in some cases are more valuable in training than in practice, and also the time taken to create such systems. Future software development will certainly provide teachers – the school's subject experts – with the opportunity to use easily manipulated software to create in-house expert systems which can be programmed in such a way as to reflect the school's curriculum and cope with the different abilities of pupils, but the creation of an expert system is a very time-consuming process because of the amount of information needed to cope even with simple questions from pupils. In expert systems, the knowledge base is provided by the expert and the information in the system is organized by a *knowledge engineer*.

For school librarians, expert systems may provide a dual opportunity. Already prototype expert systems such as MICROTEXT have been used as guides for library users in that they help the users in locating information in the library. In Stirling University, for example, MICROTEXT is used with law students using government publications. In this way, such systems may be seen as 'expert' but are partly remedial in nature. Future expert systems, designed and organized by school librarians may provide pupils with a microcomputer which is an expert in answering their information inquiries. Such a system may allow pupils to enter the library, ask the microcomputer for 'something on flight' and then be interrogated by the system. The microcomputer may ask the pupil for her/his form, what particular part of the curriculum the inquiry relates to, what purpose the pupil has in the inquiry (e.g. information for an assignment) and then ask the pupil questions about how much the pupil already knows about this topic – does s/he know any relevant keywords. The pupil will, in a very short time, be provided with actual information sources or with bibliographic information. As school librarians are OPOs (one-person operations), they cannot deal with all potential inquirers and it may be that expert systems of this type may be very useful.

The other potential use of expert systems in which the school librarian may be involved is in the role of knowledge engineer i.e. the person in the school with the training and expertise to organize the information on the expert system. School librarians will be able to create subject-specific expert systems by tapping the knowledge of the school's subject teachers. The teacher and the librarian will probably be able to work together at the microcomputer and create a small knowledge domain and dictionary of key terms and input details of the curriculum and expected learning outcomes of pupils studying that part of the curriculum and thereby produce a school-based system which can be used by pupils. It will be necessary for the school librarian to have the skills to interpret the teacher's knowledge and structure the database within the expert system. Expert systems are still in their infancy but would appear to have the potential of using microcomputers to provide new methods of teaching and learning in schools.

Compact disks and videodisks
The possibilities of using microcomputers with a range of peripheral

devices to extend the educational use of microcomputers can be seen by examining the future potential of linking microcomputers to compact and videodisk. Compact disks are now quite common in the home to produce quality sound systems and many musical recordings are now available on compact disk. Compact disks also have the capacity to store huge amounts of information. Jack Schofield in *Computer Guardian* (28.11.85) estimates that a compact disk could hold 600 megabytes of data which is 'equivalent to a hundred million words of text or 300,000 sheets of A4 paper or 2,000 novels'. The compact (audio) disk is linked to the microcomputer by a CD-ROM chip. The possibilities for school librarians of compact disks are wide ranging. It may be possible in future to buy complete reference works or encyclopaedias on disk; external databases may sell one year's database on disk, avoiding the need for regular subscriptions; library materials such as local newspapers or magazines could be stored on disk and the whole catalogue of the school and perhaps that of the local school library service could be held on a disk. The problems with present CD technology is that disks can only be read by the microcomputer but future developments are likely to provide the facility for information e.g. the library catalogue to be written on to the disk and amended at will. Problems in retrieving information in a variety of ways also still have to be resolved.

Videodisk technology also provides exciting possibilities. The ability to store and retrieve large amounts of text *and* video frames will allow future schools to provide pupils with interactive video learning whereby the pupil can use the microcomputer to access not only information in the form of text or graphics but also videorecordings. Thus a pupil studying the HEART could access written information on the biology of the human body, graphic displays of the heart but also videorecordings of the heart actually working or of operations on the heart. This ability to link a variety of sources could be used with expert systems to provide truly interactive learning by pupils. Practical constraints of cost and the time taken to create interactive video presentations will obviously limit their applications but with falling prices in technology and more sophisticated hardware in the future, these constraints may be less daunting.

The future role of the school librarian
All the above changes in technology will obviously mean some changes in the roles of school librarians and teachers. Teachers will have to become more technologically orientated in pursuing the

individualized learning goals which schools will increasingly adopt. Each new technological advance will have to be evaluated in educational terms and the potential value to a changing curriculum. As pupils prepare for a society in which work and leisure is increasingly dominated by technology, teachers will have a part to play in preparing pupils for their future roles.

School librarians will also become more involved with changing technologies. As schools become more technology and more information-orientated, the training and skills of the school librarian are likely to become more important. The school librarian may be charged with the responsibility of keeping staff up to date with changes in hardware and developments in software; may be more involved in in-service work with teachers in the applications of new technology; will be seen by pupils as the principal intermediary between them and the internal and external databases available within or through the school library; and may adopt new titles, such as school information manager or information systems manager or information resource manager. Whatever the title, school librarians will still be heavily involved in ensuring that whatever changes take place in technology, the information skills of pupils keep up with such developments. A pupil working with an expert system will still be involved in identifying purpose, in finding, using and presenting information. The technology may help but without the basic learning skills, the outcome may be that pupils will assimilate information but *learn* very little.

The future role of the school librarian is an exciting one and will require an attitude which is based on educational principles, which is prepared for change and which is, above all, flexible.

References
1. Kelly, A. V. ed., *Microcomputers and the curriculum*, Harper and Row, 1984, 168.
2. Chambers, J. A. and Sprecher, J. W., *Computer-assisted instruction: its use in the classroom*, Prentice Hall, 1983.
3. Stonier, T. and Conlin, C., *The three Cs: children, computers and communication*, Wiley, 1985.

Bibliography

Akers, N., 'Hands on at Hucknall', *SLG News* (10), Autumn 1984, 25–7.

Beck, J., 'Information technology for school children,' *IFLA Journal*, 10, (2), 1984, 145–50.

Bell, G. H., *SIR and teacher based research*, British Library, 1984.

Berglund, P., 'School library technology,' *Wilson Library Bulletin*, 59, (5), January 1985, 736–7.

Bream, L., 'Microcomputers', *Emergency Librarian*, 12, (3), January–February 1985, 41–7.

Burton, P. F. and Petrie, J. H., *Introducing microcomputers: a guide for librarians*, Van Nostrand Reinhold, 1984.

Chamber, J. A. and Sprecher, J. W., *Computer assisted instruction: its use in the classroom*, Prentice Hall, 1983.

Chandler, D., *Young learners and the microcomputer*, Open University Press, 1984.

Chen, C. C. and Bressler, S. E., *Microcomputers in libraries*, Neal Schuman, 1982.

Clyde, L. A. and Joyce, D. J., 'Computers and school libraries,' *COMLA Newsletter*, (45), September 1984, 2, 14.

Clyde, L. A. and Joyce, D. J., *Computers and school libraries: an annotated bibliography*, Volumes 1 and 2, Alcon Library Consultants, 1983 and 1985.

Costa, B. and Costa, M., *A micro handbook for small libraries and media centres*, Libraries Unlimited, 1983.

Daines, D., *Databases in the classroom*, Castle House Publications, 1984.

Davison, S., 'Computerized information retrieval in the school resource centre,' *School Librarian*, 33, (3), September 1985, 210–12.

Drexel Library Quarterly, 20, (1), Winter 1984: special issue on new technology in school library media centres.

Gilman, J. A., *Information technology in the school library resource centre*, Council for Educational Technology, 1983.

Herring, J. E., 'Information skills and information technology', *Forum for the Discussion of New Trends in Education*, 28, (2), Spring 1986, 54–7.

Herring, J. E., 'The microcomputer in the school library project (MISLIP),' *SLG News*, (10), Autumn 1984.

Herring, J. E., *School librarianship*, Bingley, 1982.

Herring, J. E. and Condon, J., *Managing school library services*, RGIT, 1986.

Irving, A., *Study skills across the curriculum*, Heinemann, 1985.

Kelly, A. V. ed., *Microcomputers and the curriculum*, Harper and Row, 1984.

Laurie, P., *The joy of computers*, Hutchinson, 1983.

McKee, B., *The information age*, Forbes Publications, 1985.

Maddison, A., *Microcomputers in the classroom*, Hodder and Stoughton, 1982.

Matthews, S., 'The computer as a resource for learning,' *School Librarian*, 32, (4), December 1984, 331–3.

Miller, I., *Microcomputers in school library media centres*, Neal Schuman, 1984.

Papert, S., *Mindstorms*, Harvester Press, 1981.

Rowbottom, M. and Templeton, R., 'Getting started: a guide to using the microcomputer in the library,' *Library Micromation News*, Special Issue, 1985.

Rowbottom, M. *et al. The schools information retrieval (SIR) project*, British Library, 1983.

Rushby, N. J., *An introduction to educational computing*, Croom Helm, 1979.

School Libraries Group, *The microelectronics revolution and its implications for the school library*, School Libraries Group, 1981.

Stonier, T., *The wealth of information*, Thames/Methuen, 1983.

Stonier, T. and Conlin, C., *The three Cs: children, computers and communication*, Wiley, 1985.

Talab, S. R., 'Copyright, microsoftware and the library media centre', *School Library Media Quarterly*, 12, (4), Summer 1984, 285–8.

Terry, C. ed., *Using microcomputers in schools*, Croom Helm, 1984.

Troutner, J., *The media specialist, the microcomputer and the curriculum*, Libraries Unlimited, 1983.

Williams, D. A. and Herring, J. E., *Keywords and learning*, RGIT, 1986.

Williams, D. A., Herring, J. E. and Bain, L. M., *The microcomputer in the school library project (MISLIP)*, Phase 1 – 1983–85, RGIT, 1986.

Appendix 1
Software list

COMMUNITEL – Communitel Ltd.
EDFAX – Tecmedia Ltd.
EDLIB – Addison-Wesley Ltd.
EDWORD – Clwyd Technics
FACTFILE – Cambridge Micro Software
FLEET STREET EDITOR – Mirrorsoft Ltd.
GRASS – Newman College
INFORMATION SKILLS – Akersoft, 16 Wensleydale Close, Nottingham
KWIRS – School of Librarianship and Information Studies, RGIT, Aberdeen
LIBRAFILE – Wilson Software
MICROQUERY – Advisory Unit for Computer Based Education
MICROTEXT – Acornsoft Ltd.
MICROVIEWDATA – Tecmedia Ltd.
MODIFIABLE DATABASE – Synergistic Software
ORDERIT – Right On Programs
PROTOKOL – Wilson Software
QUEST – Advisory Unit for Computer Based Education
SCHMIDT FILE – Akersoft
SIR – For information on the SIR program, contact British Library, Research and Development Division
SPELLCHECK – Beebug Retail Ltd
VIEW, VIEWINDEX and VIEWSTORE – Acornsoft Ltd.

Appendix 2
Glossary

Bit – the smallest component of information handled by a microcomputer

Byte – made of up of eight BITS, a BYTE represents one character stored in the microcomputer e.g. a letter or number

CAI – Computer assisted instruction is the use of the microcomputer for teaching and learning, utilizing mainly drill and practice programs

CAL – Computer assisted learning is similar to CAI, with the microcomputer used interactively by pupils and teachers

Compatibility – the ability to use software written for one type of microcomputer on another type

CPU – the central processing unit is the heart of the microcomputer, which controls all its functions

CPVE – Certificate of pre-vocational education

Database – an organized collection of information which can be added to or searched on the microcomputer

Download – to transfer information from an external source (e.g. a mainframe or microcomputer) on to the user's own microcomputer

Floppy Disk – the type of storage device used with most microcomputers. 'Floppy' refers to the flexibility of the disk

GCSE – General certificate of secondary education – new examination system in England and Wales

Hard Disk – a storage device used on a microcomputer capable of holding much larger amounts of information than a floppy disk. A hard disk is not flexible

Input – to enter (put in) data on to a microcomputer

Interface – a device to connect parts of a microcomputer system and allow them to interact

147

Mainframe – the largest type of computer, kept in a computer room and requiring permanent staff to operate it

Menu – a list of options given to a user when using certain software. The user chooses which options s/he requires

Minicomputer – smaller than a mainframe but normally with a larger memory size than a microcomputer

Modem – Modulator-Demulator – a device which connects the microcomputer via a telephone to other computers

Network – a group of microcomputers linked together within one building or in a particular geographic area

OPAC – On-line, public access catalogue – usually driven by a hard disk unit, it allows computerized access to all library stock

RAM – Random access memory – the part of the microcomputer's memory in which information may be input, deleted or changed

ROM – Read only memory – the part of the microcomputer's memory which can only be read, but not added to, deleted or changed

16+ – Courses developed in Scotland to meet the vocational needs of students in the 16-18 years range

Sort – to arrange records in a file in an order of the user's choosing e.g. numerical, alphabetical

Standard Grade – Scottish examination system designed for 14- to 15-year-old pupils

TVEI – Technical and vocational educational initiative – government sponsored scheme to encourage more pupils to choose technology-oriented courses and careers

VDU – Visual (video) display unit – a monitor displaying computerized information on screen

Appendix 3
Print-out from the SIR program (BBC version)

A) FIND GARLIC
```
   1        4 Ingredients = GARLIC
S1          4 = GARLIC
```

FRIED CHICKEN
```
   1        3 Recipe name = CHICKEN
   2        3 Ingredients = CHICKEN
S2          3 = CHICKEN
```

FIND GARLIC/AND/CHICKEN
```
   1        4 Ingredients = GARLIC
   2        3 Recipe name = CHICKEN
   3        3 Ingredients = CHICKEN
S3          2 = GARLIC/AND/CHICKEN
```

Record number 4

Recipe name
Chicken and Bacon Paté

Ingredients
50g (2oz) butter
100g (4oz) sliced pigs liver
100g (4oz) chopped gammon
100g (4oz) cold cooked chicken
1 garlic clove
2 tsp brandy or dry sherry
2 tbsp fresh double cream
salt and pepper to taste

Method
Melt half the butter in pan. Add slices of liver and gammon. Fry gently 7-10 mins. Remove from heat, mince finely with chicken and garlic. Stir in brandy/sherry and cream. Season to taste. Transfer to serving dish and smooth top with knife. Melt remaining butter and pour over paté. Chill before serving. Serves 4

Dairy Book/Home Cookery

B) FIND SHIP ★
    1   1 Keyword(s) = SHIPPING
    2   2 Title = SHIPS
    3   10 Keyword(s) = SHIPS
S1   11 = SHIP ★

FIND WAR ★
    1   1 Title = WAR
    2   6 Keyword(s) = WAR
    3   5 Bibliographic
              description = WARD
    4   2 Keyword(s) = WARFARE
    5   6 Bibliographic
              description = WARNE
    6   1 Title = WARPLANES
    7   1 Keyword(s) = WARPLANES
    8   3 Title = WARSHIPS
    9   4 Keyword(s) = WARSHIPS
   10   1 Title = WARSHIPS?
S2   19 = WAR ★

SELECT 2
S3   6 2

FIND S1/AND/S3
S4   0 = S1/AND/S3

FIND S1/AND/S2
S5   3 = S1/AND/S2

Record number 4

Title
Book of transport

Bibliographic description
Ward Lock Ltd., 1981: ISBN 0
7063 6141 5: DC 380.5

Author(s)
RUTLAND, Jonathan
TUNNEY, Christopher
KERROD, Robin
WILLIAMS, Brian

Keyword(s)
Book, Ships, History, Sail, Steam, Ferries, Cargo ships, Submarines,
Railways, Trains, Diesel, Electric, Underground, Narrow gauge, Future,
Cars, Aircraft, Jets, Jumbos, Helicopters, Planes, 8, 9, 10, 11, 12, 13

Index